CRIMINALIZATION OF BLACK, TRANS INDIVIDUALS FOR SEX WORK

ABSTRACT

This study examines the intersection of systemic racism and transphobia in the criminal legal system by analyzing the criminalization of Black, trans individuals for sex work. While doing so, I explain how the stigmatization and policing of Black, trans sex workers reflects racist, transphobic fictionalizations of Black and trans bodies as inherently sexually deviant. I further explain how these fictions are rooted in the U.S.'s history of White supremacist colonization. After recording, transcribing, and analyzing the oral histories of four Black, trans individuals who have been criminalized for sex work, I discern four main themes regarding their experiences and insights. These themes include patterns of systemic racism and transphobia that increase their likelihood of relying on sex work for survival, direct forms of violence perpetrated by agents of the criminal legal system, *in*direct forms of violence perpetrated by the system, and the various institutional, social, and political changes necessary to secure the safety and rights of Black, trans sex workers. This study reveals the criminal legal system as an institution which functions less as an arbiter for justice than an institution that forwards the biopolitical interests of hegemonic society. By disciplining non-heteronormative bodies, in this case those of Black, trans sex workers, the criminal legal system reinforces White, cis-heteropatriarchal dominance and maintains marginalized communities' positions at the bottom of the social hierarchy.

TABLE OF CONTENTS

CHAPTER I

INTRODUCTION

In the United States, Black, trans persons are criminalized and cycled through the criminal legal system at disproportionately high rates compared to their White and cisgender counterparts (Fitzgerald et al., 2015; Grant et al., 2011; and Nadal et al., 2014). Such a discrepancy illustrates the pervasion of systemic racism and transphobia in the criminal legal system. By analyzing oral histories of Black, trans persons criminalized for sex work, this study reveals the intersecting roles of racism and transphobia in the process of sexual policing, which Fischer (2022) defines as "the targeting and legal control of people's bodies and their presumed sexual activities." Specifically, as this study demonstrates, the stigmatization and policing of Black, trans people reflects racist, transphobic fictionalizations of Black and trans bodies as inherently sexually deviant (Davis; 1986; hooks, 2014; Ritchie & Jones-Brown, 2017; and Stryker, 2006) - fictions which are rooted in the U.S.'s history of White supremacist colonization, and are essential to White, cis-heteropatriarchal dominance (Currah, 2022; Ferguson, 2003; Lugones, 2008; Mogul et al., 2011; Ngu, 2020; and Snorton, 2017).

The sexual policing of Black, trans sex workers, and those stigmatized as such, positions the criminal legal system as a mechanism through which biopower is exercised (Foucault, 1990). By disciplining public displays of non-White, non-cisgender embodiment, the criminal legal system functions as a regulatory institution which fosters the life of dominant (White, heteropatriarchal) society by disallowing that of marginalized groups. Despite their disproportionate representation in rates of arrest for prostitution and related crimes, there is a dearth of research which focuses specifically on the criminalization of Black, trans folk for sex work and the relevant anti-Black and anti-trans biases at play. As such, this study asks the following questions. First, what are the experiences of Black, trans individuals who are criminalized for sex work by the U.S.'s criminal legal system? Second, and more specifically, how do they see racism and transphobia informing their experiences with the criminal legal system? And third, how do their experiences reflect or contradict broader scholarship on Black, trans experiences? These questions allow me to gain in-depth understandings of the participants' experiences with sex work criminalization. Considering the lack of research on the specific criminalization of Black, trans people for sex work, gaining such insight will allow me to build a foundation upon which future research can be conducted.

Literature Review and Theoretical Frameworks

Although there is little extant work that focuses solely on the topic of Black, trans individuals being criminalized for sex work, there is extensive research on the criminalization of a variety of demographic groups for sex work that sheds light on the specific experiences of Black, trans folk criminalized for such labor. For example, research demonstrates that queer and trans people are targeted by police for sex work at high rates due to deeply ingrained trans- and homophobia in the criminal legal system (Nadal, 2020). With regard to trans people in particular, research finds that trans folk are profiled by police as sex workers at significantly higher rates than their cisgender counterparts (Rosentel et al., 2020). Additionally, trans women are profiled as sex workers much more frequently than other in the trans community, such as trans men, nonbinary people, and gender nonconforming people (Amnesty International, 2005). These profiling practices betray the presence of transphobia in the criminal legal system, particularly with regard to stereotypes of trans people as sexually deviant and promiscuous (Ritchie & Jones-Brown, 2017).

The transphobic sexualization of transness and non-normative gender presentation is rooted in European colonialism. In the course of European colonization in North America and Africa, White Europeans encountered various other cultures that had matriarchal, multiple gender, and other non-heteronormative systems already in place (Lugones, 2008 and Mogul et al., 2011). Viewing these cultural gender formations as "savage" and "uncivilized," White Europeans upheld and imposed a strict binary as their gender system by framing gender as a product of dimorphic, biological sex (Currah, 2022 and Lugones, 2008). Moreover, they imposed a cis-heteropatriarchal social system whereby heterosexuality and male dominance was seen as the only natural, default mode (Butler, 2006 and Stryker, 2006). As heterosexuality and cisgender identities were viewed as the default, any other gender or sexual identities/representations were seen as ontologically false for misrepresenting a supposed objective reality (Butler, 1988). This perception of deviance in trans embodiment is illustrated historically by accounts of European colonizers encountering two-spirit Indigenous Americans to whom the Europeans referred to as "berdache," roughly translating to "homosexual man" or "male prostitute" (Hunt & Moodie-Mills, 2012 and Mogul et al., 2011). Europeans equated gender formations outside of their Western norms to sexual deviance in a way that disparaged and diminished the two-spirit individuals' gender presentations. During and following European colonization of North America and the formation of the U.S., dominant members of White, cis-heteropatriarchal society established a multitude of laws that regulated gender presentations and prohibited non-heteronormative expressions (Ferguson, 2003 and Mogul et al., 2011). "Masquerade laws," for example, which began in the 1800s and criminalized cross-dressing or gender-bending, equated wearing attire not associated with a person's perceived gender to an act of lewdness deserving of legal punishment (Nadal, 2020). In other words, trans people's practice of wearing clothes they saw as appropriate for their gender identity was deemed inherently sexual and therefore not suitable for public display.

The contemporary interpretation of transness as inherently sexual and deviant is a further extension of hegemonic society's conflation of gender and biological sex, and its conceptualization of heterosexuality and cisgender identities as the natural default. Because of this conflation, trans identities are viewed by dominant society as conscious choices some people make in order to attract same-sex partners and participate in "unnatural," homo-erotic sex (Anzani et al., 2021; Butler, 1988, 2006; and Stryker, 2006). Recent examples of gender non-normativity being perceived as intentional, sexual deviance include the contemporary outcry over "transgenderism" as a harmful ideology and trans people as sexual predators targeting children and youths (Luneau, 2023 and Tensley, 2022). For merely existing, trans people are being equated to terrorists whose aim, rather than living as their authentic selves, is to indoctrinate that nation's people into a world of harmful sexual deviance (Padgett, 2022 and Roos, 2022). Furthermore, hegemonic society's stereotypes of trans persons as sexually deviant manifest in the form of sexual policing whereby trans people are commonly profiled as sex workers by agents of the criminal legal system (Amnesty International, 2005; Nadal, 2020; and Rosentel et al., 2020).

The profiling of trans individuals, especially trans women, as sex workers means increased interactions with police who believe them to be participating in sex work (Rosentel et al., 2020), resulting in harmful effects for the trans community because of the typically negative nature of interactions with law enforcement. Data show that trans people frequently have negative interactions with police that entail transphobic harassment and disrespect, with rates of negative interactions ranging from 29% (Grant et al., 2011) to 57% (James et al., 2016). Qualitative research, such as that reported by Hereth (2023), finds that interactions with law enforcement are overwhelmingly negative and are most likely to result in dissatisfaction in police (Saunders & Kirby, 2010). These negative interactions make trans people less likely to rely on police for help, resulting in increased risk of harm when victimized or in times of crisis (Nadal et al., 2014), thus widening a disparity between the purpose of law enforcement and crime victimization rates (Serpe & Nadal, 2017).

People of color, particularly women of color, undergo similar discriminatory policing practices to trans folk and are profiled as sex workers by police more often than White women (Ritchie & Jones-Brown, 2017), resulting in disproportionately high rates of stops and arrests for prostitution and related crimes (Fischer, 2022; Nadal, 2020; and Ritchie, 2013). Such racial disparities in sexual policing demonstrate the effect of institutionalized constructions of Black bodies as hypersexual and deviant. The sexualization of Black bodies in the U.S., like that of trans identities, stems from the racist constructions of blackness established in European colonialism dating back to the fifteenth century. Because European colonizers brought with them cultural ideals of cis-heteropatriarchal dominance, this resulted in an emphasis on the societal importance of eugenic racial reproductivity (Fischer, 2022). Moreover, since women were seen as sites of reproduction, both biologically through birth and culturally through child-rearing and socialization, White womanhood was elevated in status as the anchor of sexual morality and the cornerstone of White, cis-heteropatriarchal social order (Snorton, 2017). As White femininity became the standard against which non-White women's racialized genders and sexualities were judged, so too did White masculinity become the standard for non-White men (Cisneros, 2013; Davis, 1986; and hooks, 2014). As whiteness became valorized as the ideal form of heteronormative patriarchy, the genders and sexualities of people of color, particularly Black people, were denoted as *non*-heteronormative and therefore inadequate (Ferguson, 2003). To further reinforce the construction of Black bodies as non-heteronormative, European scholars and colonizers created biological classifications of race that were used to justify the colonization, enslavement, and subjugation of non-European peoples (Omi & Winant, 2015). Those biological classifications, which persist even today, included phenotypic sex differences between racial groups, such as the idea Black people inherently promiscuous and have an insatiable, immoral sex drive (Robinson, 2015 and Stacey & Forbes, 2021). As a result, the sexualities and gender expressions of Black people came to be thought of as excessive and predatory in nature (Fakunle & Smiley, 2016). For Black men and people assigned male at birth (AMAB), this meant being confronted with violent victimization by those who feared they would rape all the White women (Davis, 1986). Meanwhile, for Black women and people assigned female at birth (AFAB), this meant exclusion from the realm of true (White) womanhood and allowed for the social justification of their objectification and rape (Snorton, 2017 and Spillers, 1987). Black bodies are still stereotyped as hypersexual and non-heteronormative, as evidenced, for example, by the excessive profiling of people of color, especially Black people as sex workers.

The results of such disproportionate policing practices are overwhelmingly negative outcomes for women of color who are saddled with a criminal record that precludes them from acquiring and maintaining employment and from accessing myriad public benefits (Alexander, 2020 and Fitzgerald et al., 2015). Trans women of color face even greater rates of profiling and policing for sex work as the imbrication of their gender and racial identities compounds the racist and transphobic treatment from law enforcement (Ritchie & Jones-Brown, 2017 and Saunders & Kirby, 2010). The increased rates of profiling leads to more frequent interactions with police, most of which are negative and involve some level of disrespect or harassment from officers (Grant et al., 2011; Hereth, 2023; James et al., 2016; and Stenersen et al., 2024). As a result, trans women, especially Black trans women, are arrested for prostitution and other sex-related crimes at higher rates than their White and cisgender counterparts (Fitzgerald et al., 2015 and Nadal, 2020).

Research in queer studies, transgender studies, and Black feminism offers several examples of this transphobic and racist profiling resulting in arrests and other negative outcomes for trans people of color. For example, researchers found that trans people of color experienced such discrimination even within queer communities, as was the case with Boystown, a gay neighborhood in Chicago where White residents instituted policing policies which primarily criminalized gender and racial minorities (Rosenberg, 2017). The racism and transphobia ingrained in the community's practices was poignantly illustrated by a prostitution police sting which exclusively targeted queer and trans people of color in the neighborhood (Daniel-McCarter, 2012). In Louisiana, researchers discovered that the state's Crimes Against Nature by Solicitation (CANS) statute, a more severe version of its contemporaneous prostitution statute, was used to disproportionately target Black women, trans people, and queer folk with accusations of prostitution and led to harsher-than-normal punishments for those charged (McTighe & Haywood, 2017 and Ritchie, 2013). Furthermore, Mogul and colleagues (2011), as well as Amnesty International (2005), assembled substantial collections of statements from individuals who were accused of soliciting prostitution for simply existing as a trans person of color in a public space, or "walking while trans." Moreover, there are myriad high profile examples published in news media of trans women of color being wrongfully profiled and accused of sex work, such as Monica Jones, who was arrested for prostitution for wearing a "black, form-fitting dress," (Pochoda & Strangio, 2014) and Meagan Taylor who was profiled as a sex worker when she checked into a hotel during a trip to attend a funeral (Haley, 2015 and

"Iowa Civil Rights Commission complaint", 2016).

In addition to being profiled as sex workers, trans people of color, especially Black, trans women are disproportionately represented in the sex trade (Fitzgerald et al., 2015). Research finds that trans people in general participate in sex work at a rate of 11%, while Black, trans people participate in sex work at rates as high as 47% (Grant et al., 2011). These statistics are mirrored by those which depict the rate of participation in sex work for trans women specifically. Trans women participate in sex work at a rate of 12%, while Black, trans women participate in sex work at a rate of 42% (James et al., 2016). Edelman et al. (2015) reports similar findings claiming that both trans feminine persons and trans people of color are more likely than any other gender or racial group to participate in sex work, with more than half of each group having done so at one point in their lives. The overrepresentation of trans people of color in sex work is due largely to extensive racist and transphobic employment discrimination in the U.S. Research points out that as many as 44% of trans people report being denied employment due to their gender identities, with Black and Latine trans persons facing the highest rates of job loss and employment denial due to their gender identities (Edelman et al., 2015 and Grant et al., 2011). Furthermore, trans people face extensive transphobic harassment in the workplace, which often forces them to quit their jobs (James et al., 2016 and Rosich, 2020). These types of adverse job outcomes greatly increase the likelihood that a trans person of color will participate in sex work out of necessity (Hunt & Moodie-Mills, 2012 and Nadal, 2020), with Fitzgerald et al. (2015) finding that those who face transphobia in the workplace are almost three times more likely to engage in the sex trade than those who do not. Further research finds that the increased participation in the sex trade not only places trans people of color at higher risk of interacting with police but makes them more likely to face violence at the hands of police.

Sex workers have reported experiencing myriad forms of violence from police, including, but not limited to, verbal harassment, physical assault, and sexual violence (Amnesty International, 2005; Saunders & Kirby, 2010; and Sherman et al., 2015), and research illustrates a direct correlation between high rates of policing and elevated rates of these forms of violence (Deering et al., 2014). Furthermore, sex workers have been demonstrated to be significantly more likely than non-sex workers to be subject to violence by law enforcement. For example, researchers find that, among trans people, those who participate in sex work are nine times more likely that their non-sex working counterparts to report physical attacks by police and are up to three times more likely to be raped or sexually assaulted by officers (Fitzgerald et al., 2015 and Stenersen et al., 2024). Other research similarly finds that participation in the sex trade is one of the strongest predictors of sexual violence by police (Stinson et al., 2020). These data on sex workers' elevated risk of violent victimization by police also reveal greater risks for sex workers of color, especially Black sex workers, who are significantly more likely than their White counterparts to be confronted by police (Stenersen et al., 2024). This racist pattern persists in the trans sex work community as well, as research finds that Black, trans sex workers face higher rates of interaction, harassment, and abuse from law enforcement than their non-Black counterparts (Fitzgerald et al., 2015).

Current literature in transgender and ethnic studies details the frequent profiling of trans people and people of color as sex workers, noting that individuals at the intersection of those identities are profiled even more intensely. Further, the research shows that such profiling leads to increased numbers of police interactions, which in turn contribute to higher rates of harassment and violent victimization these individuals face at the hands of police. In addition, various authors and researchers demonstrate the connection of those policing practices to racist and transphobic cultural constructions and stereotypes that originate from European colonization and the imposition of White, cis-heteropatriarchy. My study supplements the current literature by providing in-depth accounts of the experiences of Black, trans individuals who have been criminalized for sex work, thus illustrating the effects of racist and transphobic policing practices in greater detail and providing insight that other academic scholarship lacks. Moreover, I offer analyses which elucidate the systemic racism and transphobia at play in the criminal legal system, their connection to White, cis-heteropatriarchal ideals rooted in colonialism, and how they manifest in the oppression of my participants and other Black, trans people who do sex work or are stigmatized as such.

This study primarily relies upon queer of color critique, critical transgender, critical criminologist, and Black feminist theoretical frameworks. Queer of color critique draws from Foucault's (1990) formulation of biopolitics which he defines as the institutional interventions and regulatory controls over the mechanics of life (i.e., propagation, health, birth, mortality, and the conditions that cause them to vary). These interventions, Foucault asserts, give hegemonic society access to the body and power over life so that it can regulate and maintain social hierarchies. Roderick Ferguson (2003), a founder of queer of color critique, extends Foucault's theory of biopolitics, applying it to the socio-cultural regulation of queer, Black bodies such that those bodies are relegated to a permanent lower class whose existence is necessary for the preservation of capitalist institutions. Ferguson analyzes how the intersection of racial, gender and sexual practices antagonize or conspire with the normative tendencies of Western, capitalist society, and asserts that Western gender and sexual norms are conceptualized with the White body in mind and impressed upon Black bodies to justify the latter's subjugation and reinforce the former's dominance (Cacho, 2012). The racialized sexual and gender presentations of Black bodies do not properly conform to cultural standards which valorize whiteness, meaning Black bodies are regarded as innately non-heteronormative, hypersexual, and deviant.

It is from this perspective that C. Riley Snorton's (2017) work on the multiple intersections between blackness and transness emanates. Using hermeneutic analyses, Snorton juxtaposes Black and trans embodied experiences against hegemonic gender constructions that have historically excluded non-White bodies (Currah, 2022). In doing so, he exposes how Black, trans individuals subvert social expectations by merely existing, thus positioning them as always already deviant. I apply these insights to my study to understand how participants' racial and gender identities interact to situate them outside of White, cis-heteronormative ideals and mark them as targets for racist, transphobic policing practices.

To further aid in understanding the construction by hegemonic society of trans identities as deviant and subversive, this study utilizes a critical transgender theoretical framework. The theory of performativity, first posed by Judith Butler (1988, 2006) and later adopted by critical trans theorists (Stryker, 2017 and Stryker, 2006), suggests that gender is a historically situated social construct that is performative in nature. In other words, one does their gender according to scripts that change over time depending on the historical context of the culture in which said gender is being perceived. Accordingly, gender in Western contexts is erroneously seen as precipitating from one's biological sex. Gender is therefore considered innate, immutable, and binary. Thus, when performing a gender that does not correlate to their biological sex, trans people are seen as intentionally deviant, and their identities, ontologically false. Butler (1988) also extends Foucault's theories of biopolitics (1990) and disciplinary power (1995) and applies them to the subjugation of non-normative gender presentations. According to her, hegemonic society deploys various forms of regulatory mechanisms, such as the criminal legal system, that discipline non-normative presentations to "correct" their deviance. Such discipline not only reinforces White, cis-heteropatriarchal dominance, but also disallows life for non-normative populations and cements their position at the bottom of hegemonic social hierarchies. By extending these concepts to my study, I more effectively reveal the role of racist, transphobic policing practices in asserting White, cis-heteropatriarchal norms.

The critical criminological framework also makes use of Foucauldian philosophy and attempts to explain why the criminal legal system so readily penalizes non-normative sexual and gender presentations. Within the framework, conflict theory holds that hegemonic society defines what constitutes criminal behavior (Ruggiero, 2022), allowing it to promote White, heteronormative life while impairing non-heteronormative life such that the latter remains subjugated. In other words, this theory posits that crime is constructed along racialized gender lines as a mechanism for exerting socio-cultural control over non-normative bodies and disallowing their life (Foucault, 1990). Through this biopolitical lens, the criminal legal system is denoted as a regulatory institution whose primary function, rather than the achievement of justice, is the discipline of non-normative bodies and the maintenance of hegemonic hierarchies.

The historical dimension of this study, whereby respondents' experiences are juxtaposed against other works and narratives that illustrate Black, trans experiences, is guided by a Black feminist theoretical framework. I draw upon the insights of Black feminist theorists, such as Marquis Bey (2016), who explains that the knowledge the Black body has of itself is vastly different from the knowledge the "White gaze" has of the Black body. White observers of blackness, upon suppressing and invisibilizing public expressions of blackness, create epistemologies of the Black body that contradict its complexity. Bey asserts that this fabricated knowledge of blackness is a "script" imbued in Black bodies through White, cis-heteropatriarchal colonial processes. Other Black feminist researchers, such as Tia Gaynor (2018) and Hortense Spillers (1987), refer to the concept of scripts as social constructions or an "American grammar," respectively. Ultimately, they all refer to the historicization and fictionalization of Black bodies as they are interpreted via a hegemonic lens through which they are always already deviant, violent, and guilty. This framework allows me to elaborate the connection between the sexualizing subjugation of Black bodies, particularly those that are also trans, and racist, transphobic ideals asserted by White, heteronormative, hegemonic society.

Methodology

I utilized an oral history methodology which stems from historical and ethnographic research traditions, which are used extensively in Ethnic Studies. These traditions prioritize the valorization of individual experience as well as an exploration of the cultural, political, and historical contexts in which those experiences are constituted (Creswell & Poth, 2018). Likewise, the oral history approach used here emphasizes the importance of firsthand experiences and juxtaposes them against broader socio-political contexts in order to reveal the operation and function of certain social constructs; in this case, those constructs being race and gender and their role in the oppression of marginalized persons. Qualitative approaches, such as the oral history, are uniquely valuable in this situation because they allow the researcher to record first-hand experiences to ascertain the scope of the problem (Creswell & Poth, 2018), thus building a foundation upon which future research may be conducted.

The phenomenological nature of the oral history approach is ideal for this particular study due to the current state of research on the Black, trans community. Due to extensive and systemic racism and transphobia, the voices and perspectives of Black, trans folk are often silenced legally, culturally, and politically, meaning their stories seldom get expressed in mainstream channels. For example, trans people have reported experiencing high rates of abuse or lack of aid from law enforcement (Gyamerah et al., 2021 and Witten & Eyler, 1999), with trans people of color reporting significantly higher rates of abuse than their White counterparts (Fitzgerald et al., 2015), thus reducing their likelihood of reporting crime victimization to police. Crimes against trans people are hence underreported, meaning there is a lack of data pertaining to their experiences of victimization. Furthermore, there is a dearth of quantitative data on trans individuals in the criminal legal system. Organizations, such as the FBI and the Bureau of Justice Statistics, rarely, if ever, acknowledge the existence of trans people in their published crime statistics. The Uniform Crime Report (UCR) and the National Incident-Based Reporting System (NIBRS), for example, only denote "male" and "female" as sex categories and give no information about subjects' gender identity. Research has shown that despite spearheading the movement for queer rights (Burgos, 2020), trans people of color and their unique concerns are often sidelined as White, cisgender, gay men are centered in mainstream queer politics (Havey, 2021; Hollibaugh & Weiss 2015; and Rosenberg, 2017), a pattern which illustrates pervasion of racism within the LGBTQ movement (Ferguson, 2019 and Stryker, 2008). Finally, there is a lack of research into sex work that specifically focuses on Black, trans individuals.

Various studies on the topic of sex work, such as those discussed previously, emphasize the fact that queer and trans people of color in general face more severe criminalization for sex work than their cis-het and/or White counterparts, with some mentioning Black, trans people in their results. Few, however, focus solely on Black, trans individuals or the effects and intersections of transphobia and anti-Black racism. As stated previously, the oral history methodology provides in-depth understandings through the analysis of firsthand experiences and situates respondents' experiences in a historical context, thus allowing me to more effectively connect their experiences to constructs such as White, cis-heteropatriarchy and provide a level of insight of which other methodologies fall short. Oral history methodology, however, precludes me from generalizing the data. Therefore, following narrative and ethnographic traditions, the aim of this study is instead to gain an in-depth understanding of the lived experiences of the Black, trans community in relation to the criminal legal system. In doing so, I'm able to reveal the systemic nature of racism and transphobia within the criminal legal system, as well as how the system functions to socially regulate non-normative communities.

I present data obtained from eight interviews with four self-identified Black, trans individuals who have been criminalized for sex work, regardless of whether or not they were conducting sex work at the time of their criminalization. In order to protect their identities, the participants are referred to with pseudonyms. The participants - Grace, Olivia, Violet, and Faith - are all Black, trans women whose ages range from early twenties to mid-forties, all of whom are former sex workers who participated in some form of in-person sex work. Three of them (Grace, Olivia, and Violet) report having been street sex workers at some point in their time in the sex trade, meaning they solicited clients from a public space, and all four report having solicited clients through online apparatuses at some point. Grace participated in the sex trade in a Southern state, while Violet and Faith participated in sex work in different parts of the East coast. Olivia, meanwhile, conducted sex work in a state in the Western region of the U.S.

The participants were contacted and recruited through a variety of methods, most of which involved introduction through what Sanders (2006) refers to as gatekeepers, individuals who are connected, and provide access, to members of the sex work community. Gatekeepers may occupy formal positions, such as health specialists or service providers that interact with sex workers, or informal positions, such as friends, family, or other community members. I was introduced to Violet and Faith through Kim, a formal gatekeeper who works professionally as an advocate for sex worker rights but is not a sex worker herself. In my early attempts to recruit participants, I reached out to several organizations that provide services to sex work, including the one for which Kim works, to inquire about people who may be potentially interested in participating. Kim was one of the few people who responded to my inquiries and, after some correspondence and discussion of the study, agreed to introduce me to people who qualified for participation and who she believed would be interested in my research. Among those she introduced me to, Violet and Faith were the only two who responded and agreed to participate in the study. Grace was introduced to me by an informal gatekeeper, Jordan, who is a member of his city's ballroom community of which she is also a part. I met Jordan through my personal involvement in the Black, queer community, which has a significant presence in the ballroom scene in the U.S. After attending an event held for members of the Black, queer community in Denver that Jordan also attended, I introduced myself to him and mentioned my research. He noted that he knew someone who qualified for the study and would likely be interested in participating (Grace), then introduced me to her at a later point. After interviewing Grace, she introduced me to another potential participant (Olivia) with whom she has a close personal connection.

Interviews were scheduled following brief introductory meetings with each participant, during which I explained the purpose of the study, their rights as participants, and the structure of the research process. Participants were contacted for further interviews when necessary to collect further data and clarify statements, and most participants took part in multiple interviews. Olivia was the only participant who only took part in one interview because she was unable to be contacted for further discussion. The interviews themselves were relatively unstructured and progressed according to the unique themes that arose in conversation with the participants. Over the course of the interviews, I inquired about the participants' histories in sex work, their interactions with the criminal legal system, and how their experiences were shaped by racism and transphobia, both from agents of the criminal legal system and others. The interviews, which were conducted via virtual meetings and phone calls, were recorded, transcribed, and thematically analyzed to reveal themes and patterns relating the participants' experiences to the broader context of systemic racism and transphobia in the criminal legal system. Further analysis involved the juxtaposition of participants' experiences against broader scholarship on Black, trans experiences with sex work criminalization.

This study's methodology involves several different ethical considerations, such as maintaining the privacy of the participants as well as ensuring that the research contributes to the destigmatization of sex work and those involved with the industry. Sanders (2006) denotes the latter as a necessity for gaining the trust of people involved with the sex industry, thus gaining access to their stories. However, though gaining trust by establishing a clear intent and value position at the beginning of research is a necessary step, it presents a quandary in the form of potential bias as knowledge of my beliefs and goals may have affected the respondents' statements. Furthermore, I must acknowledge the role of my own positionality as a Black, trans individual. Acknowledging my identities before the participants was essential to gaining their trust to speak with me, with some openly expressing that they would not have participated in the study if I had not been Black or trans. However, this positionality presents another way in which bias may be introduced into the research. Therefore, throughout the research and writing process, I had to be consistently mindful of my biases - as do all researchers - and how they were communicated, such that the respondents were influenced as little as possible.

Maintaining participant privacy is extremely important for two reasons. First, given that the topic of sex work involves criminalized activities, respondents risk putting themselves in legal jeopardy by sharing their stories. Second, during the research process, participants and members of the Black, trans sex work community expressed concerns regarding racist or transphobic individuals who seek to harm community members by doxxing or "outing" them. As such, participants' names, locations, associates' names, and associated organizations' names have been anonymized and replaced with pseudonyms where applicable.

Finally, to avoid confusion, I elucidate here various terms I use extensively in this study that are either uncommon in their broader usage or have many disparate definitions. I use the term "criminal legal system" throughout the study rather than "criminal justice system" to refer to the institution in question because, as has been established, this work asserts that the criminal legal system functions less to enact justice - a social good - and instead works to exercise social control according to hegemonic norms and social hierarchies. Additionally, given the rapidly shifting political landscape when it comes to questions of gender and sexuality, terms delineating queer and trans identities are frequently changing and are often contested even within the communities in question. As such, I offer operative definitions for those terms I deem as necessitating clarification. This study utilizes Stryker's (2017) definition of "transgender (trans)," which refers to those who "move away from the gender they were assigned at birth." Specifically, this term is used here to refer to those who self-identify as any gender which differs from the gender category constructed and assigned to them by their culture. It should be noted that this study's sample only includes trans women as no persons of other trans identities volunteered to participate. Despite the lack of other trans identities, however, the study refers to Black, trans folk in general rather than only Black, trans women in sex work because the questions posed to respondents referred to all Black, trans sex workers. Likewise, though respondents occasionally about Black, trans women specifically, most of their statements referred to Black sex workers of all trans identities.

The term "queer," is colloquially used to refer to all those under the LGBTQIA+ umbrella, which includes trans people. For the sake of clarity, however, this study uses "queer" to refer specifically to individuals who do not identify as trans but fit elsewhere under the LGBTQIA+ umbrella. This includes cisgender people with queer sexual identities and gender non-conforming people who do not identify with the trans label. I make this distinction to more clearly delineate stereotypes and forms of oppression that are specific to the transgender experience and are not necessarily shared by all who identify or are perceived as queer. Furthermore, I clarify here the operational definition of "sex work" used by this study because the term is commonly used to refer to a wide range of occupations, such as pornographic acting/modeling, stripping, erotic dancing, and sugar babying (Nadal et al., 2014 and Stenersen et al., 2024). While this study does occasionally address these varied forms of sex work, it is primarily concerned with a specific, criminalized form of sex work. Thus, when using the term "sex work," this study specifically refers to those forms of sex work which are criminalized in the United States, particularly commercial sex (i.e., prostitution). This study uses the term "sex work" instead of prostitution because the former carries less stigmatizing connotations than the latter and reinforces the idea of sex work as a valid form of labor (Fitzgerald et al., 2015 and Saunders & Kirby, 2010). When the term "prostitution" is used, it is only in reference to laws, statutes, and charges that deploy the term.

Chapter Structure

This study's structure consists of four chapters, each elaborating on different themes that arose during interviews with the participants. Chapter one analyzes the social, political, and economic conditions which pushed the respondents to participate in sex work. The chapter demonstrates how Black, trans people, who face extensive racism and transphobia in the workplace, are more likely than almost any other racial and gender group to be forced to participate in sex work for survival. The necessity to rely on sex work in turn makes them more likely to encounter police and thus suffer the negative effects of becoming involved with the criminal legal system, such as being unable to find employment or access public benefits. In this chapter's analysis, I explain how systemic racism and transphobia, in both the workplace and the criminal legal system, function as biopolitical mechanisms that push Black, trans folk into unlivable conditions in which they must rely on methods of survival that place them in even more difficult situations. By doing so, these institutions reinforce White, cis-heteropatriarchal dominance and trap Black, trans folk at the bottom of the social hierarchy. Chapters two and three delve further into the forms of harm individuals, especially Black, trans folk, face when encountering the police and reveal examples of both direct and indirect violence perpetrated by the criminal legal system.

Chapter two explains the various ways in which agents of the criminal legal system (mostly police) directly inflict violence upon sex workers in the form of harassment, false accusations, excessive punishments, and abuse, all of which are typically experienced at higher rates by Black, trans sex workers than their White and cisgender counterparts. Harassment by police often involves victims being yelled at, cussed out, misgendered, dead-named, called slurs, threatened with arrest, or unnecessarily searched by officers, regardless of whether they are participating in sex work at the time of the encounter. Participants also report frequent experiences of false, or otherwise unfounded accusations, from police, including but not limited to lying in reports and testimonies, using condoms as evidence for arrests, and arresting individuals doing non-criminal activities in certain public spaces. Abusive actions by police cover a wide range of behaviors that include verbal abuse in the form of insults and slurs, physical abuse in the form of beatings and shootings, and, most common, sexual abuse in the form of sexual harassment, rape, and exchanging sex for leniency. Many of these acts are committed with impunity by officers as survivors are met with doubt and even animosity upon reporting their victimization. Police perpetrated abuse operates as a biopolitical strategy to impose state power for the social regulation of non-heteronormative bodies. Furthermore, the socio-political environment that protects police from facing accountability works to reinforce uneven power dynamics between law enforcement and sex workers, the unevenness of which is even further exacerbated for Black, trans folk because of the inherently racist, transphobic nature of the criminal legal system.

Chapter three elaborates on the indirect types of violence imposed upon Black, trans sex workers, identifying sex work diversion programs, placement in men's jails, and the inability to rely on law enforcement as the most significant forms of indirect violence reported by participants. In this chapter, I explain how diversion programs not only harm sex workers by violating their rights, but also by taking a hyperindividualistic approach to confronting social issues. By focusing on the choices and proclivities of individual sex workers, diversion programs encourage us to turn away from systemic issues of racism and transphobia pervading the criminal legal system that ultimately harm marginalized communities. The criminal legal system also presents harm indirectly to Black, trans sex workers by incarcerating them with men, which places them in dangerous situations as research demonstrates that Black, trans people, especially Black, trans women, face extremely high rates of physical and sexual assault when placed in men's pods in jails and prisons. Finally, I explain how their inability to rely on law enforcement for fear of persecution or police victimization places Black, trans sex workers at high risk of encounter victimization from others due to how often they are targeted for crimes. Those who seek to victimize sex workers, either through robbery, physical assault, sexual assault, or some other form of violence, frequently target Black, trans folk because they are aware the police are not likely to care. The institutionalization of hegemonic norms which promote White, heteronormativity deprives Black, trans sex workers of a vital safety net which many others are able to enjoy: the criminal legal system. By denying them protection, the criminal legal system puts them at increased risk for violent victimization, thus reinforcing their oppression and the dominance of White, cis-heteropatriarchal society.

Chapter Four expounds upon various changes, reforms, policies, and movements necessary to ensure greater safety and public health for Black, trans sex workers highlighted by participants. Included are calls for educational efforts that destigmatize sex work, law enforcement policy reforms, legislative proposals, decriminalization of sex work, and abolishment of the prison industrial complex (PIC). Some of these approaches, such as the educational efforts, policy reforms, and legislative proposals, reflect dominant perspectives on the criminal legal system and place emphasis on individual actors rather than addressing broader systemic issues at the root of the problem (i.e., racist, transphobic carceral logics that emphasize punitiveness and social control over public health). Others, such as decriminalization and abolition, promote public health over all else and focus on the deconstruction of White, cis-heteropatriarchal norms that reinforce racist, transphobic social hierarchies. With these analyses,

I explain why the latter are more effective approaches for promoting the safety and wellbeing of Black, trans sex workers.

CHAPTER II

PATTERNS OF INVOLVEMENT

During a seminar I attended in the Spring of 2023, titled *Ask Me Three Questions*, four panelists talked at length about the intersection of ballroom culture, sex work and the Black, queer community. One of the panelists, Shanae Adams, explained to the audience how sex work as a profession provided necessary support for the ballroom scene, a historically queer, Black space. According to Shanae,

> when we talk about the movement for Black Lives Matter, when we talk about Ballroom experience and how sex work intersects, sex work funded the movement. You know, the majority of people who are working in these houses, who are funding these balls, who are putting their children, providing a roof and shelter for their children to be able to live in, they're engaging in survival sex work, which is a particular form of sex work in which you're just trying to get your basic needs met.

I begin with this story to highlight the crux of this chapter, which is the understanding of sex work as a survival strategy for people unable to rely on legal forms of employment, especially those individuals in marginalized communities. My study's participants likewise recite the sentiment that sex work is a useful strategy employed by members of marginalized communities when unable to find gainful legal employment. Grace emphasizes that trans people today still face extensive systematic oppression which makes it difficult for them to find and maintain legal employment. Hence, sex work offers a promise of survival. Violet claims that, since Black, trans folk are less likely than others to receive government assistance, they are more likely to rely on sex work. Extant data bear out these realities, showing, for instance, that Black and trans individuals alike are more likely than almost every other group to receive government assistance (DeSilver, 2023 and Henris, 2023). Moreover, trans folk commonly face difficulties when trying to apply for public benefits due to both individual and institutionalized transphobia. According to the Center for American Progress, trans people face difficulties when providing identifying information because it may contain inaccuracies if they changed their name to match their gender. Many trans people also reported to the Center that they face hostile treatment from government staff, and some expressed they had intentionally neglected applying for assistance simply to avoid being confronted with discrimination (Henris, 2023). Furthermore, existing research highlights the disproportionate representation of Black and trans people in rates of poverty, homelessness, and unemployment, considered some of the greatest risk factors in terms of one's likelihood for participating in the sex trade (Edelman et al., 2015; Fitzgerald et al., 2015; Fraser et al., 2019; Grant et al., 2011; Hunt & Moodie-Mills, 2012; James et al., 2016; Nadal et al., 2014; and Rosich, 2020). Thus, even though Black and trans folk are more likely to receive government assistance than their counterparts, their overwhelming representation in poverty rates makes Black, trans individuals more likely to turn to sex work for survival. One of the largest contributors to poverty rates among Black, trans individuals is racist and transphobic employment discrimination.

In this chapter, I demonstrate how employment discrimination, resulting in poverty and unemployment, pushes trans individuals, especially Black, trans folk, out of their workplaces and toward sex work as a survival mechanism. Additionally, other factors, such as lack of community support and racialized, gendered fetishization, increase the likelihood of Black, trans individuals turning to sex work for survival. Finally, I explain how the reliance on sex work for survival, caused by the various listed factors, increases one's risk of becoming involved with the criminal legal system, thus placing them in greater danger and reinforcing their need to rely on sex work.

Discrimination, Sex Work, and Survival

Three of the four participants in my study explicitly communicate that they entered the sex industry out of a need for survival. Grace states, "I grew up in that time where, as a young, transgender, Black woman, people were not hiring us…." According to her, sex work was "the easiest way to ensure that your bills were getting paid and that you had a roof over your head." Unable to rely on her family for support from a young age, Olivia describes having turned to sex work as a way of "taking care of [herself]." Violet expresses that she originally began sex work because she was following the examples of her peers who "seemed like they were having fun" while doing sex work. That changed for her, however, and she describes being placed in a position of needing it for survival. "When I had to do it for survival," Violet states, "it became very tough. It became very dangerous because it was so many trans women that were getting robbed, raped, and even murdered." Despite the evident danger, sex work became a necessity for survival for Grace, Violet and Olivia.

While Faith claims that sex work was not a necessity for her survival, as it was for the other women, her experiences largely overlap with the reasonings given by the other participants. She recalls barely getting by with the legal employment she held prior to engaging in sex work. She was working while putting herself through school, and despite working all the hours she was able while still maintaining her academics, she was only making $200 per week. Living paycheck to paycheck, she could only afford the bare essentials and nothing more. Sex work proved to be more lucrative and also offered Faith an escape from the transphobic discrimination she faced in the workplace. While sex work was not an absolute necessity for Faith's survival, she was unable to maintain what most would consider acceptable living standards, thus necessitating her participation in the sex industry.

In the participants' experiences, the employment discrimination they faced as Black, trans individuals was one of the primary reasons they turned to sex work for survival. Grace describes at length the various forms of employment discrimination with which she was confronted. Oftentimes, she would be barred from acquiring legal employment at all. She describes being "looked over completely for someone who was cis or someone who was less qualified than [she] was, but who happened to not be trans." Grace strongly suspects that transphobia played a part in her rejection from potential employers and describes encountering myriad transphobic microaggressions from potential employers, as well as direct statements that she was not being given the job due to her gender identity. This aligns with other trans individuals in the sex trade who have had similar experiences of more subtle discrimination, such as applying for a position they had been told was open, only to be turned away when employers discovered they were trans (Nadal et al., 2012)

Grace's experience of being denied employment for her gender identity is not an anomaly, and broader scholarship on employment discrimination reveals patterns of transphobia and racism (Kattari et al., 2016). The National Transgender Discrimination Survey (NTDS), for example, found that 44% of survey respondents reported being denied jobs due to their identities as trans. On top of being denied new employment, 26% of all respondents reported job loss due to gender identity/expression; Black (32%), multiracial (36%), and Native American (36%) people experienced much higher rates of job loss than the average. This goes some way to explaining the finding that trans people of color experience unemployment at four times the national average rate (Grant et al., 2011). Edelman et al. (2015) reported similar findings in their report on the Washington, D.C. Trans Needs Assessment. In that study, 40% of trans people reported being denied jobs due to their gender identity, with Black (45%) and Hispanic (46%)

respondents reported higher rates than White respondents (30%). NTDS respondents also reported being outed during interviews and immediately denied employment, as well as going from relatively high paying positions to minimum wage following gender transition (Grant et al., 2011). James et al. (2016) also recorded several statements from trans survey respondents who explained how they were fired as soon as they came out as trans or struggled with unemployment since beginning gender transition. In these studies, it is clear that being out to one's coworkers/employers plays a significant role in the attainment and retention of employment. Testimonies in the works of Grant et al. (2011), James et al. (2016), and Nadal et al. (2012) all noted that issues with finding and keeping jobs began or intensified following the discovery of respondents' trans identities. Notably, such was the case in Faith's experience.

When she was younger, at a time when she was struggling to find legal employment, Faith was afraid of being discovered as trans; for her, "everything was a secret." She went to great pains to hide her status as trans because she knew being out would negatively impact her employment in two primary ways. First, she would frequently be fired from or outright denied positions by employers because of her gender identity. These instances usually involved more subtle forms of discrimination, such as those discussed earlier, where employers would find unreasonable, albeit technically legal, excuses to deny her just after discovering she was trans. Second, being out as trans negatively impacted her employment because of the rampant discrimination she would experience after being outed. She recounts working as a parking attendant at a mall where her male coworkers would sexually harass her by constantly flirting with and making unwanted advances on her. This continued until she was outed as trans to the entire workplace by one of her coworkers, at which point the harassment became overtly hateful and even more dangerous.:

> I remember: my mailbox, my name was scratched off and my real, you know, my dead name, was written on there .... That was like the most embarrassing moment of my life, and then from there it was just chaos ... just you know little hate notes, whatever, you know, dirty looks, whatever, and all that nature ...

The harassment Faith faced from other employees became so severe that she soon quit her job in order to escape the discrimination.

Her decision to quit in order to avoid harassment and potential violence is one commonly made by other trans folk in the workforce. The United States Transgender Survey (USTS) found that 15% of trans respondents made the choice to quit their jobs in order to avoid discrimination in the workplace. Testimonies from the survey detail respondents feeling uncomfortable being out as trans in their workplaces and taking significant pay cuts in order to work somewhere they felt safe (James et al., 2016). Trans people of color quit their jobs to avoid transphobic discrimination at even higher rates and James et al. (2016) found that Black, trans individuals did so at a rate of 19%, 5% above the rate at which White, trans folk, quit their jobs to avoid discrimination. Thus, even when able to attain jobs, Black, trans folk too often find themselves forced to quit due to the severity of the discrimination they face for their identities. Some of my study's respondents experienced many forms of such discrimination firsthand.

On one occasion, while working for an employer and openly identifying as a trans woman, Grace used the women's restroom during her shift. As she left the stall and began washing her hands, an elderly, White woman entered the restroom and used one of the stalls. Thinking nothing of it, Grace went back to work, but shortly thereafter found that the woman had reported her to the manager of the establishment and claimed that Grace had attempted to peer at her over the stall. The manager immediately believed the customer and apologized rather than attempting to get Grace's side of the story. In another instance, when Grace worked for a different employer, she describes events that transpired while staying at a hotel on a several week-long business trip where she oversaw the training of other employees. While she was off the clock, she invited a man who she met on an app to her room. When the man later left, one of her supervisors, whom she described as a "zealous Christian woman," saw him leave and immediately caused a stir which almost resulted in Grace being kicked off the training team:

> she made it a big deal, like, basically she was trying to make it like, the only reason that a transgender woman would want to be on a job where she gets to travel with work is so that she can be a slut, basically. Like, that was her premise of everything.

The discriminatory nature of the supervisor's accusation is further emphasized by the fact that many cisgender women on the business trip were also inviting men to their rooms whom they had met at clubs or bars during off-hours. Sometimes the women would also have other employees come to their rooms. However, Grace was the only person on the team reprimanded for the same behavior. Grace confirms that she suspected her supervisor was trying to imply that she was engaging in sex work while on the business trip, despite the fact that Grace was not. In this example, stereotypes of Black, trans women as promiscuous jeopardized Grace's employment. By merely existing as Black and trans, one becomes stigmatized as a sex worker, which, in turn, makes it more difficult for members of that community to maintain stable, legal employment.

Although this situation was resolved, Grace was eventually fired from her position at the company because that same supervisor witnessed her being gifted marijuana by another employee on her birthday (recreational marijuana had not yet been legalized in her state). The supervisor only witnessed the receipt of the gift because she had been spying on Grace through a peephole during Grace's break on a shift. Her supervisor's racist and transphobic perception of Grace as deviant by nature was used to justify inappropriate surveillance and find excuses to fire her. She is not the only participant in my study to have withstood such invasive behaviors in the workplace.

Faith, in a similar example, recounts an experience in which she was accused of "fraternizing with a client" at her workplace, a non-profit where she helped clients with housing concerns. One of Faith's clients, who had just reintegrated back into the community after spending thirty-three years in prison, eventually felt comfortable enough with her to confide in her about more personal matters. He expressed having issues being intimate with his wife due to erectile dysfunction that developed during his years in prison. Wanting him to get the help he needed, Faith referred him to medical services that could offer him aid, all the while recording the interaction in progress notes which her supervisors were able to review at any point. Later, she was called into a meeting with her supervisors where she discovered one of her coworkers had overheard part of the conversations with her client and reported her for having an inappropriate relationship with him. Rather than reading the progress notes or doing anything to confirm the veracity of the claims, the supervisors immediately assumed that Faith was indeed being intimate with a client and confronted her with their concerns. Faith felt strongly at the time, and even now, that the stereotype of trans people as promiscuous and licentious individuals negatively affected her employer's perception of her character, thus leading to discriminatory practices. Grace and Faith's experiences demonstrate a pattern of stereotyping where trans women are perceived as hypersexual. This stereotype, coupled with the perception of Black individuals as always already guilty of deviant behavior, fosters an environment in which the hyper-surveillance of Black, trans folk is considered justified. Instances of wrongdoings, whether real or imagined, are then used to confirm racist, transphobic biases in the workplace. In short, Black, trans folk face a cycle of workplace discrimination whereby bias fabricates deviance, which then deepens bias.

Similar to the testimonies of trans folk in the works of Grant et al. (2011), James et al.

(2016), and Nadal et al. (2012), Grace and Faith's experiences of transphobia in the workplace were partially dependent upon whether their colleagues knew of their identities as trans. Knowing that being out as trans in the workplace posed risk, respondents in my study developed strategies to keep their identities hidden. They emphasize the importance of being able to "pass," or to be perceived by others as the gender which one is attempting to appear as. Faith, at one point feared being known as trans, and as such put great effort into her appearance and presentation in order to "blend in" and go unnoticed by others. After others in her various workplaces discovered that she was trans, she was then regarded as someone they perceived as flagrantly disregarding gender norms, thus making her a recipient of transphobic discrimination.

While Faith had confidence in her ability to pass, Grace had some difficulties doing so. She states,

> so I only had like a little, you know, I don't know, like an A-cup breast and I've always been a tall, wide girl. So I've always felt like that looked very awkward, you know, like no hips, no ass, you know, like those kind of things were very… they were very important to getting a job because without them, either you knew for a fact that people were only focusing on the fact that you were trans or that was what you convinced yourself, you know?

Because her lack of access to gender affirming care (GAC) negatively impacted her ability to pass as a cisgender woman, Grace was placed at greater risk of encountering transphobia in her workplaces. Grace also expresses that by being unable to pass, she was often perceived by others as being unable to "correctly" display femininity. Her supposedly inadequate display of femininity elicited harmful, discriminatory behaviors from others that functioned as attempts to "correct" her gender expression. Following a Foucauldian philosophy of social power, Judith Butler (1988) asserts various social systems employ disciplinary mechanisms that work to enforce conformity to hegemonic gender norms. This is to say, in response to trans folks' perceived deviance from gender norms, discriminatory behaviors work to enforce conformity to those norms. In Grace and Faith's cases, social discipline for gender deviance took the form of employment denial or discriminatory workplace practices. On multiple occasions, they were treated with contempt and suspicion by colleagues and supervisors whose disdain was derived from stereotypes as Black and trans people as promiscuous, irresponsible, and dangerous.

To avoid such disciplinary mechanisms, trans individuals use various tools to pass and adequately conform to gender norms, one of those being GAC. While forms of GAC, such as hormone treatments, significantly affected the participants' abilities to pass, access to GAC depended largely on socio-economic status. Faith indicates that when she was young and first transitioning, acquiring hormone treatments was extremely difficult because estrogen injections were $279 per bottle and each bottle would only last about two months. Some who weren't able to access professional medical care bought hormones from underground markets for $50-100 per bi-weekly injection. Some of the underground sellers were scammers selling placebo injections. Grace recalls how trans people in her area would occasionally have to travel out of state or even out of the country to acquire hormone treatments.

Given the obstacles to acquiring hormones for GAC, it comes as no surprise that those living in poverty or with low incomes have a harder time finding treatment than those with higher incomes. Faith notes that a disparity in access to hormone treatment also existed along racial lines due to the difference in average socio-economic positions between Black and White trans folk. In her experience, though all trans folk experience difficulties from transphobia, White, trans individuals tend to be better off financially than Black, trans folk. This aligns with existing data which show wealth disparities between Black people and White people in the United States. For instance, Black and brown populations are relegated to low-wage positions compared to their White counterparts (Gaynor, 2018), illustrated by data from multiple studies.

The U.S. Census Bureau found that, as of 2022, Black households have the lowest median income ($52,860) compared to every other racial group (Guzman & Kollar, 2023). Likewise, the U.S. Department of Labor found that Black people have the second lowest average weekly earnings ($791.02) compared to other racial groups ("Earnings Disparities by Race and Ethnicity," n.d.). In addition to these racial wealth disparities, trans people of every racial category earn less on average than their cis counterparts. Edelman et al. (2015) found that 57% of trans people of color make below $10,000 per year and James et al. (2016) found that Black trans folk lived in poverty at a rate of about 38%, more than three times the rate of people living in poverty in the U.S. adult population at the time of the survey (12%). Economic insecurity is even worse for those Black, trans individuals in the sex industry, with as much as 50% of that group making less than $10,000 annually in household income (Fitzgerald et al., 2015).

These racial wealth disparities are largely the result of systemic racism. Following the manumission of slaves, White southerners began to see Black people as competition in the labor force, which led to a shift from Black people being viewed as docile and submissive, to violent and dangerous (Fakunle & Smiley, 2016). Furthermore, Black liberation meant a loss of labor that was once free. Thus, in response to the perceived threat to White supremacy, those in power took steps to criminalize the Black population with the Black Codes and Jim Crow laws, resulting in the incarceration of Black people en masse who could then legally be enslaved under the Thirteenth Amendment (Alexander, 2020; Davis et al., 2022; and hooks, 2014). Weaponizing the criminal legal system worked to stunt the upward mobility of the Black population and largely relegate them to the lower class. This racist history of anti-Black criminalization in the U.S. is partially to blame for the wealth disparity between the Black and White population. Redlining, acts of mass violence, and other efforts which largely prohibited the accumulation of generational wealth in Black communities were also primary contributors to the current wealth disparity (Alexander, 2020). Taken together, these histories help to explain the racial disparity in access to GAC.

Rather than focusing on financial disparities, Olivia emphasizes the effect of stereotypes surrounding the intersection of blackness and queerness as the reason why Black, trans folk have a harder time acquiring hormone treatments than White, trans people in her city. Various racist stereotypes work to exclude people of color from the normative ideas of queerness and transness. Patel (2019) asserts that the hegemonic ideal of White supremacy is present in queer communities as it is in heteronormative culture. As such, racial differences are denied in favor of racial homogeneity and queer people of color are excluded from mainstream representations of queerness (Giwa & Greensmith, 2012). Similarly, Rosenberg (2017) holds that racism has played a significant part in the creation of queer urban spaces, meaning that queer people of color are often classified as Other and excluded from such spaces. This exclusion of people of color from queer culture is born partially from racist stereotypes that paint Black and brown bodies as incapable of "correctly" performing socially accepted forms of gender or sexuality (Logie & Rwigema, 2014). It is also grounded in homonormativity, a tendency in queer culture to adopt the normative and exclusionary practices characteristic of heteronormative culture (Stryker, 2008). Homonormativity is a neoliberal politics of "large-scale consumerism and national allegiance" (Rosenberg, 2017, p. 139) that promotes the production of a normative, commodifiable subject (i.e. cisgender, gay, White men).

In other words, rather than attempting to change the systemic, intersectional oppression affecting all queer identities, homonormative queer culture seeks to carve out a spot for itself in hegemonic society (Ferguson, 2019). As a result, mainstream queer culture adopts normative practices and participates in exclusionary practices that exclude Black and brown people from the category of queer. The hegemonic ideal of queerness is a White subject, thus invisibilizing queer people of color and, as Olivia states, adding an extra "hoop to jump through as a black trans person to even just get an appointment" for GAC. She explains that Black people are sometimes not seen as able to be queer and the validity of their queer identities is questioned. In her experience, health care professionals are influenced by homonormative ideals and sometimes prohibit Black, trans folk from accessing GAC because the professionals deny their transness which they view through a racialized lens. As a result, some Black, trans individuals have their prescriptions denied or are dissuaded in office visits and therapeutic sessions from getting GAC. Due to health care disparities, and the aforementioned wealth disparities, Black, trans people have less access to GAC than White ones. Seeing as passing provides, to an extent, security for trans people, this means Black, trans individuals are at greater risk of violence and harassment.

Even when provided with access to gender affirming care, however, participants' racial identities worked to further compound negative perceptions of their gender identities. Grace, Violet, and Olivia all express having been perceived by others as more masculine than their non-Black counterparts, thus making it more difficult for them to pass. The perception of these women as more masculine than their non-Black counterparts stems from racist stereotypes that code Black bodies as hypermasculine, particularly when it comes to the bodies of those assigned male at birth (AMAB). Such stereotypes are well documented. In her elaboration on the myth of the Black rapist, Davis (1986) detailed the demonization of Black men as hypermasculine savages whose sexual urges drove them to assault White women. Alexander (2020) and Stacey & Forbes (2021) likewise explain how the perception of Black men as hypersexual manifests in the criminal legal system and gay dating scene, respectively. Writers such as hooks (2014),

Snorton (2017), and Spillers (1987) all illustrate how the hypermasculinization of Black bodies also extends to those who present as feminine, detailing the historical exclusion of Black women from the normative idea of womanhood for being perceived as too tough, aggressive, and hypersexual.

Olivia puts it succinctly when she states, "...[Black] people automatically have this stigmatization that we naturally look more masculine. So, like it seems like, oh, we look less passable." Grace adds, "I felt like a lot of times because I was the black trans girl that a lot of men were... what's the right way of saying it? Like, I guess they were scared." She mentions that her clients would often perceive her as "more dominant" due to her race despite the fact that she had never before acted dominant or "masculine in any way, shape or form." Violet recounts similar sentiments from clients who specifically went to her for services because they perceived her as more masculine than other, non-Black, trans women. Perceptions of these women as masculine, and thus not as passable as their White counterparts, carry over to their places of work and mark them as targets for transphobic discrimination.

Faith, on the other hand, does not perceive her blackness as affecting her ability to pass. Instead, she attributes her pass-ability to other genetic features (e.g., face structure) as well as her knowledge of how to "blend in," which she describes as performing femininity in such a way that doesn't "stick out" and follows the norms of femininity established in a given location. Faith does note, however, that the likelihood of facing discrimination was increased by the fact that she was a racial minority in her workplace. Even when she was able to pass and avoid being outed as trans, racist discrimination would still make it harder for her to find and maintain employment than her White counterparts. The racial employment discrimination she encountered follows patterns of racial disparities in the workforce established by research which shows that

Black people in the U.S. receive lower wages than White people on average and are also more likely to experience unemployment ("Labor Force Characteristics," 2020 and Wilson & Darity, 2022).

The extensive discrimination participants faced made it extremely difficult to find legal employment that would allow them to survive. They would be turned away outright from employment opportunities for the fact of their trans identity or be given various reasons for not being offered a position that they strongly suspected were due to transphobia. When the respondents *were* able to find employment, they would encounter discriminatory practices and harassment that would either result in them being unjustly fired or forced to quit. As illustrated by my study's respondents and other research on systemic racism and transphobia, the difficulties Black, trans people face in attaining legal employment are rooted in a long history of White, cis-heteropatriachal oppression. Perceptions of trans people as deviants, Black people as aggressive, and both groups as hypersexual contribute to their exclusion from the workforce and their over-representation below the poverty line. Having no other choice, my respondents relied on sex work to provide them with financial security that legal employment would not. In other words, sex work provided a reliable method of survival, guaranteeing that they had food and shelter. Employment discrimination is not the only factor involved in pushing Black, trans people toward the sex trade, however. Lack of community support systems, such as those found in schools, families, and peers, greatly exacerbates the need of Black, trans folk to rely on sex work.

When openly identifying as trans, many experience pushback from their community support systems who often adhere to hegemonic ideals of gender and sexuality. Black communities are no different and many who identify as queer or trans find themselves rejected by their support systems and thus left without a social safety net that most others enjoy. Take Olivia, for example. She began sex work at fifteen and remained in the industry until the age of twenty. Her primary reason for turning to sex work was fear that her "heavily religious" mother wouldn't accept her for her gender identity, nor sexuality. She, explains that she "wanted a little cushion under myself, so if she did find out I had my grounds of taking care of myself." While Olivia had not yet been kicked out of her home when she began sex work, it is such a common occurrence that she felt the need to get into the industry in preparation for a potential expulsion from her home, a very likely eventuality. Violet, with her experience encountering Black, trans youth in the sex industry, confirms that Olivia's decision is not unusual for someone in her position. She claims that although some youths might not be kicked out by their families, they leave of their own accord to be able to openly identify and live as trans, something that was considered "unacceptable in [their] home." In other words, whether they are explicitly removed from their homes by their families or pressured to leave for fear of mistreatment, trans youths are often driven from their homes and support systems by hateful, transphobic beliefs and discrimination (Fraser et al., 2019; Hunt & Moodie-Mills, 2012; and Stanley & Smith, 2011).

Olivia's experience reflects the fact that queer and trans youths are at increased risk of joining the sex trade compared to their cis-het counterparts because so many of them are kicked out of their homes due to transphobia and homophobia. Queer/trans youth are disproportionately represented in the homeless population, with queer and trans youths representing up to 40% of the homeless youth population in the U.S. despite composing only 5-7% of the overall youth population (Hunt & Moodie-Mills, 2012). Considering that poverty increases the likelihood of joining the sex trade, it makes sense that there exists such a significant correlation between homelessness and involvement in the sex trade (Fitzgerald et al., 2015). This means that, being more likely to experience homelessness, queer and trans youth are increasingly likely to participate in the sex trade.

Grace notes that there are marked differences between the experiences of Black and White, trans youths who are kicked out of their homes because of the "privilege that comes along with the color of a white girl's skin." According to her, one way the privilege manifests is White, trans girls' abilities to find more business as sex workers than their Black counterparts. She states,

> I can't tell you how many times when we were working the streets, how many times we would have clients, and I'm talking about of all races and all creeds, that would, "hey, do you know where any white girls are? Hey, where can I find the white girls around here?" And every time, as a black trans woman, you hear that, it's like, what the fuck? Do you know what I mean? Like, what?

In other words, she believes that White, trans individuals are able to find more success in the sex industry than Black, trans individuals. Some existing literature supports Grace's claim. Race-based sexual stereotypes are prevalent in the queer dating scene and function to discourage heterogeneity. Queer people of color in Stacey & Forbes' (2021) research reported experiencing extensive racial fetishization on gay dating apps. The fetishization objectified the subjects and pressured them to conform to racialized sexual stereotypes. These stereotypes include the notion that queer people of color are violent, sexually predatory, or likely to have an STD (i.e. HIV). Robinson (2015) finds that such stereotypes also function to delineate queers of color as undesirable and ineligible for dating or sexual intimacy. In the sex trade, this translates to fewer people seeking the services of Black and brown sex workers, resulting in less financial stability.

The lack of support from participants' communities extends beyond the home. Olivia describes current conditions in high schools where her younger peers experience transphobic bullying.

According to her,

> a lot of even teenagers are saying like, with the GSA's (Gay Straight Alliances) being taken out and stuff, it's making it easier for them to be bullied because of their lifestyle.... And I've noticed like a lot of teenagers say like that's mostly why they are getting into the industry is because this bullying is being brought into not only in their schools, but in homes.

The GSAs in high schools in Olivia's area have been shut down due to backlash from parents who said the alliances conflicted with their religious beliefs. This pushback to the acceptance of queer and trans identities opens the way for increased transphobic bullying in schools. Various academic works support this conclusion, stating that the presence of GSAs in schools correlates with lower rates of gender and sexuality-based victimization and increased feelings of safety among queer and trans students (Heck et al., 2011 and Lessard et al., 2020). Ioverno & Russell (2020) specifically note that GSAs produce particularly protective environments for trans youths. According to Hunt & Moodie-Mills (2012), because of transphobic biases school administrators often dole out harsher punishment to trans students, even when they are the victims of bullying rather than the perpetrators. Schools will sometimes go so far as to involve law enforcement when disciplining trans students, thus shunting them into the school-to-prison pipeline. Indeed, research indicates that anti-trans victimization in schools is associated with greater odds of incarceration for trans youths (Rosentel et al., 2020), a reality which also aligns with extant research on how children of color are often pushed into school-to-prison pipeline, thus place Black, trans kids at even greater risk of becoming involved with the criminal legal system. Involvement in the criminal legal system greatly hinders one's ability to find employment and attain financial security due to the stigma of a criminal record (Alexander, 2020), therefore increasing the likelihood that one may need to rely on sex work as a profession. Olivia claims that younger and younger people are being subject to anti-trans bullying, thus increasing their chances of joining the sex trade. Her insight is reflected by contemporary research on transphobic bullying in schools which finds that trans youths experience significantly more bullying and victimization than their cis counter parts ("LGBTQ+ youth bullying effects," 2021; Sares-Jäske et al., 2023; and Underwood et al., 2020). These high rates of victimization in schools have been shown to make it increasingly likely that trans youths will rely on sex work for survival (Dank et al., 2015 and Greenfield et al., 2021). With the increasing number of minors coming out as transgender (Herman et al., 2022), this means that more youths are at risk of being bullied and having to rely on sex work.

Effects of Involvement with the System

Involvement in the criminal legal system further exacerbates discrimination faced by Black, trans individuals. For example, jails and prisons expose trans folk to extraordinarily high rates of sexual assault and rape (James et al., 2016). These rates increase even further if the inmate is a sex worker (Fitzgerald et al., 2015). Involvement in the criminal legal system makes it extremely difficult to find legal employment (Alexander, 2020 and Ritchie, 2013), which in turn makes it more likely that one will experience poverty. For Black, trans folk who already experience incredible difficulty finding and maintaining legal employment thanks to extensive discrimination, involvement in the criminal justice system can only further reinforce their need to rely on sex work for survival. All of these factors (being a sex worker, living in poverty, being Black, being trans) significantly increase the likelihood that Black, trans folk will have encounters with the criminal legal system, therefore subjecting them to further discrimination.

Those living in poverty experience significantly higher rates of incarceration than the general population (Camhi et al., 2020 and Rabuy & Kopf, 2015). Sex workers, who are more likely than the general population to be living in poverty, are also significantly more likely to come into contact with law enforcement (Fitzgerald et al., 2015). Black, trans people are disproportionately represented in the criminal legal system because of systemic, anti-Black racism and transphobia, displaying higher rates of incarceration than almost any other gender-race demographic (Grant et al., 2011 and James et al., 2016). These intersecting oppressions, evident in the criminal legal system, compound for Black, trans sex workers to create an environment where they are extremely likely to come into contact with the criminal legal system.

My participants' responses thus far reflect historical patterns of the effects of systemic racism, demonstrating that Black and trans folk are not only more likely to participate in the sex trade but are also more likely to be cycled through the criminal legal system while doing sex work due, in part, to their racialized gender identities and their over-representation in poverty rates. Grace recalls that, "the low-income areas" and workers who "[looked] like they were the low-income girls" were targeted the most by police. She explains how,

> [the police] would notice those type of things and began to harass the people that they knew were dependent and surviving off of sex work and they would try to stop that by taking us to jail, harassing us all night long so we didn't pick up any clients, pulling up-pulling clients over in the neighborhood, clients that were driving around looking like just pulling them over and scaring the bajeezus out of them. Those type of things.

The police in Grace's area were able to identify those women who were low-income and relying on sex work for survival, then went out of their way to specifically target them. They would use various tactics to limit the women's ability to conduct work, thus driving them away from an avenue for survival. Relatedly, Violet emphasizes that low-income Black communities are targeted more than White communities by the police. According to her, sex workers in low-income areas were targeted the most "because those were the ones that were out there the most, because they needed money." In other words, sex workers in low-income areas were out on the street more often thanks to their heavy reliance on sex work and were therefore more visible to patrolling law enforcement. Being so exposed to police and criminalization placed them at greater risk than their higher income counterparts of being arrested or harassed. Grace claims the classifications (and stigmatizations) of sex workers that needed the work for survival and those who didn't were largely divided along racial and gender lines. She recalls,

> so, from what I remember, a lot of the cis white women had houses and cars and they had things and they were just out there because they wanted to make the money, there was no survival necessity there for them. So, if things got hot or things got heated, they could hop in their cars and go home, you know, like they could go down the street, go inside of their house, go home. A lot of the black girls did not have that. A lot of the black girls were there also for survival.

Those who relied on sex work - commonly trans women - were not able to leave at a moment's notice, and even if they were, they would soon be back on the street and at risk of arrest because doing so was one of their only options for gaining income. Furthermore, many Black, trans women who worked the streets in Grace's city lacked a reliable means of transportation, meaning they were often unable to travel long distances for work and instead had to work near their homes. Seeing as their place of living was in the same area being policed, that made it more difficult for Black, trans sex workers to avoid encounters with law enforcement, even when they weren't working.

Faith reports that when she still conducted sex work, the poorest and most vulnerable communities in her city consisted of immigrant communities of color. These groups were comprised of people who sought asylum in the United States but were unable to find work due to lack of experience, language barriers, or being undocumented. Caribbean, Haitian, and Jamaican immigrants, for example, who struggled to find work relied heavily on sex work for survival. However, this further contributed to their already high rates of involvement with the criminal legal system and further exacerbated the racial divide between those who were and were not stigmatized as needing to rely on sex work for survival.

Creating a vicious cycle, not only do police more frequently target those who rely on sex work for survival, but involvement in the criminal legal system exacerbates the need to rely on sex work for survival. Along with the employment discrimination Black, trans individuals face because of their identities, those with criminal records are further stigmatized as deviant and delinquent. This stigmatization makes most employers less likely to see them as viable candidates for work positions (Alexander, 2020) and makes it more difficult to receive certain public benefits that could alleviate financial burdens (i.e. student loans, public housing, food stamps) (Fitzgerald et al., 2015). As Grace articulates,

> when a transgender person ends up in the system, they're in the system, and it is a very hard place to come out, and this is from experience. It's a very hard place to come out of and it- it tacks on so many things that will live you with you for the rest of your life. There's so many there. There have been times that I have... been fully qualified for jobs- fully, you know, like 100%. They wanted me the first interview, second interviews and then the background check comes and the background check shows that, oh, [Grace] had an assignation to prostitution felony charge. You know, "oh well, you know what. We don't think this is a good fit for you." So, those kind of things. Even though that was well over eighteen years ago now for me - you know what I mean?… I will say nowadays it doesn't so much because the time, so much time, has passed by, but there were many of jobs that I have lost due to the fact that- and so many of those times I thought about the fact that, like, I was literally doing nothing but minding my business when I got arrested for this. I was literally doing nothing but trying to make some money to get a hotel room, and this is how I ended up, you know, like, and eighteen years later, I'm still, I'm still, eighteen years later, being penalized. For what I had to do back when I had to do what I had to do.

As Grace's experience illustrates, the need to rely on sex work for survival, a particularly frequent reality for Black, trans folk who experience high rates of poverty, places individuals at great risk of encountering the criminal legal system.

As my participants' experiences illustrate there are various ways in which Black, trans people are pressured to take up sex work as a method for survival. As my respondents and other research have shown, extensive employment discrimination and the lack of social support systems work to make financial security and economic advancement incredibly difficult for them to attain. Black, trans people, therefore, are over-represented in poverty rates, thus making them more likely to need to rely on sex work as one of their only available sources of income. Not only are Black, trans folk at relatively high risk of becoming involved with the criminal legal system due to systemic racism and transphobia, but their odds of doing so increase dramatically if they are low-income and participate in sex work. Involvement with the criminal legal system increases the need to rely on sex work for survival as it reduces employment and welfare opportunities available to people. In other words, Black, trans folk criminalized for sex work frequently find themselves in a vicious cycle of discrimination and criminalization where they are made more and more to rely on the sex trade as their source of income.

In the proceeding chapters, I demonstrate how higher likelihood of involvement with the criminal legal system proves dangerous for the lives and health of Black, trans individuals. To do so, I detail the various ways in which the criminal legal system enacts harm and violence upon Black, trans people criminalized for sex work, by spotlighting the direct and indirect harm for my respondents and others in their communities. Direct harm includes acts such as harassment, false accusations, as well as physical and sexual abuse perpetrated by officers and other agents of the system. Indirect harm, on the other hand, includes instances in which agents of the system either deliberately put them at risk of violence from other actors, or neglected to provide adequate support when they were victimized.

CHAPTER III

DIRECT VIOLENCE PERPETRATED BY THE CRIMINAL LEGAL SYSTEM

All respondents report experiencing some form of direct harm from the criminal legal system and its agents. Such harm was most often perpetrated by police officers during their encounters with Black, trans sex workers. Among these forms of harm are harassment, false accusations, disproportionately harsh treatment, and abuse. The experiences identified as harassment most often involved the respondents being yelled at, cussed out, misgendered, dead-named, called slurs, and threatened with arrest or unnecessarily searched by officers regardless of whether they were participating in sex work at the time of the encounter. Some respondents had multiple experiences with false accusations where they were accused of participating in sex work and charged with prostitution despite there being little to no evidence they were actually doing so. Other respondents report having faced harsher charges or treatment from the criminal legal system when compared to their White and/or cisgender counterparts. Finally, respondents report various instances of abuse perpetrated against them by agents of the criminal legal system. The forms of abuse detailed in this chapter consist of verbal, physical, and sexual abuse, each comprised of several examples. In my analyses, I assert that these extralegal displays of violence, most of which are done with impunity, function as a biopolitical extension of state power that reinforces White, cis-heteropatriarchal dominance through the social, psychological, and physical disciplining of non-heteronormative bodies.

Harassment

Some actions by law enforcement are not always obviously identifiable as harassment, but constitute harassment, nonetheless. These more ambiguous forms of harassment involve officers forcing individuals to vacate public spaces, which they have the legal right to occupy, for the mere suspicion that they intend to commit prostitution, a suspicion which is often based on racist or transphobic assumptions about an individual's proclivity for deviance (Cacho, 2012 and Mogul et al., 2011). Such behavior by law enforcement most often takes the form of "move-alongs," whereby officers would interact with participants, or their clients, with the intent of forcing them to leave the immediate area, as opposed to arresting them or issuing citations. One of the least harmful forms of such harassment involved police driving up to groups of sex workers on the street, occupying public spaces, and flashing their spotlights in their faces to force sex workers to leave the area. The immediate police presence constituted a hostile environment which discouraged sex workers from meeting clients and staying in the area. Officers often do this regardless of whether they witness a person participating in sex work or not, meaning this occasionally happens to people who aren't conducting sex work at all, but simply happen to be in a high traffic area.

Occasionally, move-alongs would involve officers speaking over their PA systems to verbally harass the participants, or even brief detentions where officers would stop and question them as they were walking down the street. Violet, for example, recounts how officers would pull up to her location and immediately start bombarding her with questions such as, "'what the hell are y'all doing out here?'" Grace recalls how officers sometimes sat parked across the street, shining their lights on her until she and her friends dispersed, while at other times, they followed her as she walked, shining their spotlights on her, and speaking through their PAs for several minutes at a time. These experiences reflect established patterns of police behavior in move-alongs. In their survey of sex workers and those perceived as such in Washington D.C., the Alliance for a Safe & Diverse DC (2008) found that over half of its respondents had been told to "move along" by police because they had been profiled as sex workers. Forty of its 111 respondents had been insulted, humiliated, or verbally abused by officers. The alliance's respondents recalled being mocked and referred to as "whores" and "tricks."

In addition to insults, officers often humiliate trans sex workers by purposefully misgendering them. When being addressed or detained by police, Grace reports that officers would often intentionally misgender her to the extent that it came as a genuine shock to her to be gendered correctly by police when she moved to her current home in the Midwest. When analyzing police misconduct against queer people in the U.S., Amnesty International (2005) found that officers frequently use a names or pronouns that don't match trans people's identities, sometimes doing so intentionally in order to humiliate the person. Further adding to the harassment of misgendering, officers would dead name trans sex workers in Grace's previous city and only address them as the name on their IDs. Grace reports that officers would use the fact that her ID had a different name than her own as an excuse to stack her charges with accusations of fraud, reflecting Amnesty International's (2005) finding that when individuals produce identification that "does not match their gender expression," officers tend to view them as fraudulent or deceitful. These perceptions make it more likely that a person will encounter harassment from the police. For example, one respondent in their study, a Latina trans woman, testified to being arrested for providing false information to a police officer because her driver's license identified her as female, but the officer perceived her as male. Grace's experiences of being perceived as deceitful by officers are not aberrations and instead follow a pattern of police behavior toward trans individuals who come into contact with the criminal legal system (Hereth, 2023). As Fischer (2022) elaborates in their analysis of sexual policing, sex workers, and those stigmatized as such, are placed in an inescapable criminalized legal status because they are seen as being guilty of attempting to solicit sex for money no matter where they are. Similarly, the criminal legal system renders trans individuals unable to follow the law because their identities are constantly construed as deceitful and therefore criminal. Criminalization is thus a nearly inexorable fate for trans individuals, especially trans sex workers, because the criminal legal system is designed to target and punish deviations from hegemonic norms.

The examples of criminalization and harassment described above also follow a historical pattern of the use of overly vague laws to criminalize Black and queer for existing in public spaces. Following the end of slavery in the U.S., Southern legislators adopted the Black Codes which prompted the establishment of vagrancy laws. These laws made it a crime to not have a job and were applied exclusively to Black people. Inspired by wealthy Southern Whites' fears of losing the economic dominance they had acquired during slavery, vagrancy laws provided a way to restrict the upward economic progression of Black communities. Following the abolishment of the black codes, Jim Crow laws continued the pattern of leveraging overly broad vagrancy law almost exclusively against Black people. The laws defined activities such as "mischief" and "insulting gestures" as crimes, making it incredibly easy to justify biased arrests of Black individuals (Alexander, 2020 and Davis, 1986). Vagrancy laws from that period were the progenitors of "quality of life" policing. This form of policing emphasized maintaining social order by prohibiting behaviors that, while not outright harmful, are thought to be indicative of social deterioration in a community. Modern quality of life regulations criminalize a wide spectrum of behaviors in public spaces (i.e. loitering), such as standing, sitting, sleeping, making noise, and approaching strangers (Daniel-McCarter, 2012 and Rosenberg, 2017). They tend to be more strictly enforced in marginalized communities because the vague language of the laws lends them to biased, arbitrary enforcement.

Such laws have also historically been used to criminalize gender and sexual minorities.

For example, arrest rates of women soared in the early 1940s as many were charged with "morals offenses," which included vagrancy, disorderly conduct, and prostitution (Fischer, 2022). As Fischer points out, this explosion in criminalization rates for women precipitated from sexual policing practices which sought to reinforce hegemonic norms to attract White capital to rapidly growing urban city centers. A slew of similar laws was also weaponized against members of the burgeoning gay scene in the early twentieth century in order to expel them from public spaces and prevent large gatherings of the queer and trans communities, such as drag balls (Chauncey, 1994). Some of these laws criminalized public expression of deviant gender formations, such as laws that mandated a person's adornment of at least three pieces "gender appropriate clothing" under threat of arrest for fraud (Currah, 2022 and Stanley & Smith, 2011). Other laws, many of which operated under the auspices and rationale of sodomy laws, criminalized "cruising," or searching for sexual partners in public spaces (Chauncey, 1994). As a result, gay men were disproportionately targeted and charged with degeneracy, indecent exposure, loitering, or prostitution, often without having been caught in an overt sexual act (Nadal, 2020). The usage of quality-of-life regulations and laws against morals offenses persists today, and such laws are disproportionately leveraged against trans persons and people of color who are frequently criminalized despite not being caught participating in any overt, criminalized behavior (Mogul et al., 2011).

My study's respondents all point out a noticeable difference in the experience of move-alongs by sex workers occupying different demographics/areas of privilege. For example, Olivia explains:

> I had Caucasian trans girlfriends who also did it, and it was more like, "Oh, we're just checking on you. Have a good day." Versus me, it's like, "what's your name? Where are you coming from? What are you going to do? Can we have proof of this is where you're going?"

Similarly, Grace explains,

> I remember there being a time that there would be like three or four of us black girls on one corner, and then maybe like a Latin girl and a couple of white girls on another corner. And then maybe like a couple of white girls down the street on another corner. I remember the cops literally passing right by the white girls, right by the white Spanish girls and coming straight to the black girls' corner. And then we'd be the ones standing there with spotlights shining on us. And it was so obvious that they weren't even trying to hide it.

Both experiences speak to a racist bias on the part of law enforcement toward Black sex workers, particularly those with darker skin complexion. Violet expresses similar sentiments and explains that she would compare stories with White, trans sex workers she worked alongside, only to find out that they were not targeted for harassment nearly as often as she and that they did not feel the need to conduct their business with as much caution as their Black, trans counterparts. Likewise, Faith reports that, from her experience, White sex workers did not seem to be pulled over and harassed to quite the extent as those in the Black community. These disparities demonstrate a pattern of policing which reflects hegemonic views of Black bodies as non-heteronormative. In other words, Black bodies' racialized gender expressions constitute deviance in the eyes of the criminal legal system, thus warranting discipline. Many of the respondents' interactions with police reflect the racialized nature of gender in hegemonic society, whereby whiteness is an essential component to the hegemonic ideal of womanhood. Mogul et al. (2011) asserts that women of color are subjected to gender policing and punishment because the "cult of true [White] womanhood" necessitates their exclusion from the bounds of heteronormativity. The derision and policing of Black bodies, particularly those of women is a function of White heteronormativity. White women are rewarded for distancing themselves from "deviant" (i.e. Black) forms of femininity and thus adequately performing their gender roles according to hegemonic standards (Cacho, 2012). Grace points out one such interaction that occurred while she was incarcerated. She recalls that while she and her friends were treated poorly and frequently harassed by the corrections officers, those same officers would go out of their way to treat their White counterparts with kindness and respect, even going so far as to bring in makeup products for the White, trans inmates.

Faith points out gendered disparities between cis and trans people within the sex industry. According to her, cisgender sex workers are better able to find success as strippers, "clubhoppers," and OnlyFans models than their trans counterparts. Conversely, trans sex workers are more likely to have to be "out in the streets" where they have a higher visibility and are thus at higher risk of experiencing harassment. This reflects patterns outlined in the previous chapter which show that trans and Black people experience more difficulty finding legal employment than their cis and White counterparts due to discrimination in the workplace, and Faith reveals that such discrepancies also exist in those parts of the sex industry that are not criminalized (i.e., strip clubs, pornography, etc.).

Other participants also note a marked difference in treatment between cisgender and transgender sex workers. Grace notes that, in her experience, "black cis women did not experience nearly as much harassment from the police and from law enforcement as black trans women did." Violet also claims that when police were patrolling the streets and conducting move-alongs, "they wouldn't even look at the cisgender women. It would be all about the transgender women." This difference was also noted in relationship to passing. Grace describes an instance in which she was walking alongside another trans woman when she was accosted by an officer:

> I can distinctly remember there was a time that I was walking down a street with my girl [Sofia]. [Sofia] was five foot six, Puerto Rican girl, real slender, you know, beat, stunning, but she was trans. She was just beat and stunning, you know. And I will never forget the officer pulling in front of us on the street as we were crossing the street. He pulled in front of us and said, "Hey, you." And she thought he was talking to her. So, she was like, "What I do?" And he was like, "Oh, no, not you. You're fine, sweetie. Go

> ahead." And let her walk on and literally stopped me and went through the whole spiel and like ran my ID and the whole nine yards.

To Grace, Sofia was not subject to the same treatment because she was "passable." In this instance, Sofia, whose appearance portrayed a socially "adequate" display of femininity, was spared from harassment, while Grace, who did not pass as well as her friend, was detained. In the previous chapter, I established that the inability to pass exposes trans people to increased risk of employment discrimination, therefore making it more difficult to find and maintain work. Grace's experience demonstrates that the same phenomenon that pushes her and other Black, trans women to engage in sex work - the inability to pass - also causes the police to target them more frequently. Both in and out of the legal workplace, then, passing provides a layer of protection to Black, trans individuals that lessens the likelihood of harm. Additionally, there were notable differences in experiences of harassment based on socio-economic status. Violet states that, regardless of race or gender, a person was more likely to be harassed by police if they were part of the low-income community. This aligns with Grace's comments in the previous chapter, where she stated that officers often go out of their way to specifically target low-income sex workers because of stigmatizations of people living in poverty.

In addition to the forms of harassment detailed above, the participants also report being subject to unnecessary and inappropriate searches. Random searches are common where police line up all the sex workers in an area and search their bags for drugs, paraphernalia, and anything else they can use to make an arrest. Violet describes how officers occasionally become violent in such instances:

> they'll make them take off their wigs and all of that. Yeah. In the middle of the street, like literally make them take off their wigs, like, "take that shit off your head." Like, you know, all kinds of things. If they have false- false breasts, then make them take them out their shirt. Like, yeah, it was a lot of a lot of… humiliation going on.

As she illustrates, instances of harassment involving unnecessary searches can place sex workers at risk of further violence because they can potentially escalate into sexual harassment. Violet expresses that police justify such invasive acts by claiming to suspect the victims of criminal wrongdoing. However, their disproportionate use against Black and trans individuals, as well as the frequent lack of any overt criminal act committed prior, reinforce the notion that these inappropriate searches, rather than legitimate practices for ensuring public safety, are instead state-sanctioned forms of harassment directed at Black, trans, and sex working communities.

A throughline of the experiences iterated here is the sense that the harassment, and the women themselves, were treated by officers and other agents of the criminal legal system as spectacles. During the course of conducting this research, I was able to speak with Kim, an advocate and activist for sex worker rights on the East Coast of the U.S. While she identifies as neither Black, nor trans, and thus did not qualify as a participant in the study, her experience as a relevant expert in sex workers' rights activism provided useful insight. Kim emphasizes how the police seem particularly "enamored" with Black, trans individuals. This fixation on the Black, trans community manifests in outsiders intruding upon community space to observe and harass the marginalized group as a form of twisted entertainment. According to Kim, officers would even take White civilians on ride-alongs through Black neighborhoods simply to gawk at Black, trans sex workers on the street as if they were in a zoo. This is a form of "slumming" and serves to reinforce hegemonic hierarchies as White pleasure seekers juxtapose their social and sexual behaviors against the non-heteronormative behaviors of the (non-White) people they observe for their amusement (Heap, 2009). In the context of my participants' experiences, this means that by intruding upon Black spaces and reducing Black, trans bodies to aberrant sources of entertainment, White people and their law enforcement chaperons reinforce the dominant notion of White superiority.

The treatment of Black bodies as a spectacle is pervasive not only in the sex industry, but in a number of other environments. Mercer (1994) elaborates how Black people experience an ontological reduction whereby their characters are seen as innately, and predominantly, erotic, citing the fetishistic focus on the bodies of Black athletes, entertainers, and manual laborers. He notes that the success of Black people tends to be most socially accepted in fields which focus primarily on a person's body. Bey (2016) identifies this ontological reduction as a function of the "White gaze" which creates an epistemology of the Black body that lacks the complexity and nuance of that body. What Kim and Bey's observations have in common is that the fetishistic White gaze isolates itself from the Black body which it observes. In Bey's analysis, the White gaze fabricates a false epistemology of Black bodies because it lacks direct contact with them, a result of centuries of segregation and invisibilization of Black people. By distancing themselves from blackness in order to maintain White supremacist hierarchies, White observers of Black bodies are made to fabricate an idea of blackness that is conducive to its dominance. In this same vein, the officers and ride-along participants that Kim describes distance themselves from the Black communities which they observe, both physically with the doors and windows of the car, and socially with their White privilege and the badges that symbolize authority. The treatment of Black, trans sex workers as spectacles not only functions to reinforce notions of White supremacy, but to reduce Black bodies to stereotypes which are convenient to White hegemonic dominance.

The presence of a fetishizing, hegemonic gaze is most poignantly illustrated by one of Grace's strange encounters with an officer after meeting with a client. One night, according to her, the same officer that would spout slurs and vague threats to her over his PA system, followed her and her date to an out of the way spot. Instead of confronting them right away, however, the officer waited and watched until they had finished their business to interrupt them. The officer pulled the man out of the car and, rather than arresting him, forced the man to give him his wife's number under threat of jail time. After receiving the phone number, the officer told the wife that her husband had been caught with a "Black transvestite prostitute" before sending the man home without further punishment. Grace, on the other hand, was arrested. Rather than confronting them right away and putting a stop to their business in the first place, the officer decided to watch the entire event in hiding before embarrassing Grace's client in front of his wife. It did not escape Grace that the officer waited and watched the entire interaction before stepping in instead of intervening immediately. Once again, the distance created both physically and socially by the officer's gaze serves to reinforce hegemonic racial structures and also reveals a spectatorial enjoyment of the racialized gender policing on the part of the officer. Moreover, just as the White gaze, according to Bey (2016), creates epistemologies for the purpose of reifying racialized social hierarchies, the officer's gaze reduced Grace's identity to an object of shame (i.e., a "Black transvestite prostitute") to socially disgrace the client who ultimately got away with less punishment than Grace. Further, the officer's gaze asserted hegemonic society's biopolitical strategy of delineating non-heteronormative, Black, trans bodies as targets for punitive discipline (Ferguson, 2003), thus reinforcing the notion of the criminal legal system as a mechanism for social control (Hereth, 2023 and Fischer, 2022).

The notion that Black, trans communities are reduced to spectacles in the eyes of agents of the criminal legal system is also reinforced by a pattern that appears when exploring the different experiences in White versus Black neighborhoods. Treatment of sex workers by police is harsher and occasionally more dangerous in White neighborhoods than it is in Black neighborhoods. The respondents all express that Black communities in their respective areas were policed more than White ones, a pattern which is supported by extensive research on over-policing in Black spaces. According to Chen et al. (2023), for example, smart-phone data reveal that police spend considerably more time in Black neighborhoods, even when controlling for density, socioeconomic status, and crime-driven demand for policing. Likewise, Chalfin et al. (2020) finds that Black communities are over-policed and are disproportionately affected by the resultant arrests for low-level "quality-of-life" offenses. Not only were Black neighborhoods in my respondents' areas policed more, but when it came to the actual enforcement of laws relating to sex work, the participants express that they were more likely to face criminal penalties if they were working in White neighborhoods. In other words, when police patrolled Black neighborhoods, they were more focused on harassing sex workers than making any actual arrests. These patterns of behavior enforce segregation with the differential policing of White versus Black spaces, ensuring disproportionate impacts and more negative outcomes of policing for those residing in Black spaces. In White neighborhoods, however, a Black sex worker would almost certainly be arrested or seriously harmed, which is why Grace explains that she,

> stayed pretty much in the Black neighborhoods only because I knew that going into the White neighborhoods was nothing but trouble. And you were either going to end up sadly dead or in jail. Like there was nothing in between, you know.

According to Grace, police activity in White neighborhoods is borne out of apparent concern for those communities, whereas police activity in Black neighborhoods is simply geared toward harassing residents and flexing their power over civilians. This difference in intent behind police practices reveals the biopolitical nature of the criminal legal system. Just as Fischer (2022) explains, sexual policing in White spaces is often more severe because law enforcement's goal is to reinforce White, cis-heteropatriarchal values in order to attract White capital to the area. In contrast, sexual policing in Black neighborhoods is intended to assert White dominance and Black subjugation by criminalizing Black bodies, thus permanently relegating them to the bottom of the hegemonic social hierarchy (Ferguson, 2003; Hereth, 2023; and Fischer, 2022).

The difference in treatment between Black and White sex workers, as well as the difference in police activity in Black versus White neighborhoods, indicate that police are less concerned with public safety and more concerned with ridding the streets of Black, trans people who they see as a sort of social plague. Research shows historical patterns of criminalization intended to exclude Black and trans bodies from public spaces. Mogul et al. (2011) detail myriad laws that have criminalized public lewdness, specifically "deviant sexual acts." The lack of explicit definition of what constituted "deviant sexual acts" meant that individual officers were able to set their own standards for public decency, resulting in the disproportionate arrest of queer people in public spaces, such as parks. Furthermore, as Alexander (2020) points out, police departments insist that their public presence in the form of patrolling officers in Black neighborhoods is necessary because they believe most drug crimes are committed outdoors, despite a dearth of evidence to support this claim. The result of this persistent presence of law enforcement in public spaces, as both Alexander and Chalfin et al. (2020) indicate, is the disproportionate criminalization of Black people for quality-of-life offenses. Daniel-McCarter (2012) and Rosenberg (2017) both examine the culture and social structures of Boystown, a gay village in Chicago, and find that White residents there emphasize the need for strict law enforcement that discourages the occupation of public spaces by queer youths of color. This limits the ability of queer youths of color in Boystown to access queer-friendly public services there, thus ensuring worse life outcomes for them than their White neighbors.

As in the case of Boystown, participants in my study express feeling as though law enforcement seeks to usher them, and other Black, trans people, out of public spaces to reinforce hegemonic gender norms by delineating their gender expressions as deviant and dangerous.

Violet explains that the police in her area when she was a sex worker were trying to get trans women off the streets by any means necessary, whether by sting operations, threats, or aggressive move-alongs. The police were less concerned about what the women did or what happened to them, "they just wanted trans women off the street." Grace describes being seen by law enforcement as caged animals when she was a sex worker. Illustrating the views of the police in her previous city, she states,

> We deserved to be caged. We should have only came out at night. In the dark of the cover of night on the back roads. Otherwise, you don't exist and you're not a person. You're not, you know, you don't have human rights because we don't even see you as a human....

The harassment behavior of officers in my respondents' testimonies, as well as historical patterns of these types of behaviors, reveal that the criminal legal system, while ostensibly striving for justice and community safety, functions instead to enact social control by leveraging state power to police and punish those who dare to deviate from hegemonic gender norms (Cacho, 2012). The understanding of the criminal legal system as a large-scale mechanism for social control is further supported by the extensive evidence of fraudulent accusations and excessively harsh punishments disproportionately doled out to Black, trans sex workers.

False Accusations and Excessive Punishment

On top of harassment from officers, participants report myriad experiences of fraudulent, or otherwise unfounded, accusations on the part of officers, often accompanied by harsher than normal punishments doled out by the criminal legal system. A common justification of reasonable suspicion for officers to accost or arrest sex workers was the presence of condoms on the workers' persons. Upon spotting someone they suspected of engaging in sex work, officers would stop the person, search them, and if they discovered condoms on their person, the officers would arrest them regardless of whether or not they were actually participating in sex work at the time. For example, Grace reports,

> if you had, I believe in [the city I lived in], it was three or more condoms in your purse, on your persons, in your wallet, then it would be considered for the use of prostitution, which is just unheard of to me. What if I'm just a girl who likes to have sex and I like to be protected?

Violet reports similar experiences, stating, "if I'm walking down the street and they stop me and search my purse and they find a condom in my purse, they can arrest me." Likewise, when Faith was working for a non-profit specializing in public health and harm reduction, officers would often accost her when she was on the job handing out condoms to members of her community.

In all these instances, arrestees were charged with "assignation" or "manifestation to commit prostitution." Such statutes are meant to target attempts to solicit prostitution, meaning a person does not have to be actively engaging in sex work at the time in order to be charged. To do so, these laws must criminalize a broad range of behaviors that don't constitute prostitution. For example, behaviors such as waving at someone while walking down the street or talking to people in vehicles are considered attempts to solicit sex for money ("Prostitution," 2022). These statutes bear obvious resemblance to the previously discussed vagrancy laws. Like those laws used to criminalize the existence of Black and queer bodies in public spaces, manifestation laws criminalize behaviors that aren't harmful in and of themselves. Furthermore, they use vague language to criminalize a broad range of behaviors such that officer bias plays a significant role in determining who is punished, meaning marginalized groups are disproportionately charged under these laws (Alexander, 2020 and Mogul et al., 2011). The disproportionate effect of manifestation statutes is so profound that, in some circles, they are colloquially referred to as "walking while trans" laws (Brydum, 2014). Because trans people are so frequently profiled as sex workers, they merely need to exist in public to be criminalized under those laws.

Olivia recalls being approached by police for suspicion of violating similar statutes, despite not working at the time. According to her, police would stop her as she was walking to the grocery store or a restaurant because she had become a "known face" and recognized by officers as a sex worker. Grace and Violet recall similar experiences, and Faith points out the racist enforcement of such laws becoming an egregious issue. In a part of her city, adjacent to where the Black, trans sex work community typically conducted their work, was an area composed predominantly of Latine, Central, and South American people. Unfounded accusations of prostitution and assignation by officers were so frequent in the area that romantic couples could face arrest simply for being in public together because officers would claim that one of them was a pimp or john, and the other a prostitute. The women in that area eventually resorted to carrying their marriage licenses on their person when out in public with their husbands to avoid false allegations.

Further intensifying the disproportionate effects of assignation and manifestation statutes are certain areas designated "prostitution zones." These zones are designated by the criminal legal system as areas with high prevalences of prostitution. Assignation, manifestation, and other laws that criminalize sex work are more strictly enforced in these zones than in other neighborhoods. Faith and Grace indicate that these zones are specifically drawn out such that the designated area would have a high concentration of racial minorities, trans folk, and people living in poverty. This means that Black, trans individuals, especially those in low-income areas, are at increased risk of being confronted by police in those areas, regardless of whether or not they are participating in sex work at the time. Violet states, "because [the] area is a high-volume sex working area, you don't even have to be out there doing sex work. You could just be walking, and they'll stop you." Grace recalls one such encounter,

> I literally was leaving my friend's house to go to the store… and she lived dead smack in the middle of this zone that they had deemed the sex worker zone…. And so, there was a truck stopped at the stop sign right outside of her house. The guy asked if I wanted a ride. I said, "No, thank you, I'm just going to the store," and waved to my hand, kind of like,

> you know, a no thank you, just going to the store and kept walking. Next thing I know, I have two police cars behind me saying that I just waved this guy down trying to get his attention and that I was going to jail. Like literally walked out of the house to go to the store and got arrested.

Grace's presence in a public space was enough for her to be criminalized, demonstrating one of the ways in which the criminal legal system makes it impossible for some individuals to not break the law (Fischer, 2022). Viewed through a biopolitical lens, these zones exacerbate the hegemonic perception of non-heteronormative bodies as always already guilty, thus creating environments in which such bodies cannot possibly exist without being criminalized. By doing so, the zones function as a biopolitical tool for the criminal legal system to disallow the lives of Black, trans folk and reinforce their subjugated position in hegemonic social hierarchies.

These examples of overly broad laws being used to punish the mere existence of trans folks follow a long pattern of racist and sexualized criminalization practices. Just like the vagrancy laws of the Jim Crow era, and their predecessors in loitering and public indecency statutes, assignation, manifestation, and other similar laws function as a method of social control that reinforces gender and racial norms. Furthermore, they are disproportionately leveraged against Black communities such that some Black, trans folk even express hesitance in leaving their own homes because their public presence can be construed as overtly sexual and therefore deviant.

Occasionally, the unreasonable accusations would go beyond dubious reasonable suspicion. Violet recounts an experience where she was arrested under the pretense of manifestation to commit prostitution and the officers completely falsified their reports. Similar to Grace, she was offered a ride home by a stranger at a time when she was not engaging in sex work.

Unlike Grace, she accepted the ride and got in the stranger's car. She recalls,

> so, it's like, next thing you know, the police pull up and they was like, "Well, we got you on recorder saying that, you know, talking about price," and all this stuff, which never happened. So, yeah, I got arrested for that. I didn't do no time behind it, but yeah, I just felt that that was very wrong for them to lie just to lock up trans women.... I spent the night in jail, got out the next day. I went to court and they try to say they found - well, they said they found me guilty, but I basically fought it because I felt like, how can you find me guilty when I didn't say it? And then I was like, "Well, if you have a recording, then you need to play the recording for the court." So, they couldn't produce a recording. So, they were basically just falsifying arrests.

The officers, having a flimsy justification for reasonable suspicion in the first place, decided to bolster their accusations with lies. Upon failing to produce the alleged recording, the court had no choice but to drop the charges and Violet was released from jail.

Participants also experienced retaliation from law enforcement in the form of false, unfounded, or unreasonable charges. Retaliation from law enforcement would most often be triggered by those accused of prostitution fighting their charges. Grace recounts a time when she was caught in the middle of a weeks-long sting operation, after which she was charged with assignation to commit prostitution as well as multiple drug charges. She denied being guilty of each charge, stating that at no point did she intend to provide commercialized sexual services for the undercover officers. Regardless, she was held in jail for six months until she bonded out. With her public defender, Grace fought the fraudulent charges until they were dropped. An entire year after the ordeal, however, she found that the state had a warrant out for her arrest under the same charges. As she later discovered, her initial case was dismissed "without prejudice," meaning it could be refiled at a later date. After fighting the charges for another eight months, the case was once again dismissed without prejudice when the original arresting officer refused to show up to deposition. She claims he neglected to show up for deposition because he feared the evidence of his text conversations with Grace being released. Several months later, Grace found an officer standing outside of her building, waiting to arrest her for a third time.

She describes how,

> …the state took almost three years of my life, juggling it around and playing with it. And finally, on the third time, the judge said, I am dismissing this, this time without prejudice, which means you all will never be able to bring this up again. Because it's absolutely ridiculous. The judge was starting to see what was happening. He was starting to see through the whole shit. The state had no choice but to start seeing through the shit.

Throughout the whole ordeal, Grace's public defender revealed that the likely reason the state would not let the case go was because she chose to fight it rather than resigning to her fate within the criminal legal system. Despite having her case dismissed on three separate occasions and never being found guilty, Grace still suffered the consequences of being forced into the criminal legal system. Not only did she lose several months of her life while incarcerated or in court, but the case remained on her criminal record. As discussed in the previous chapter, a record of involvement with the system makes it more difficult to find employment and access public benefits, thus making it more difficult to escape the system.

Violet confirms that, in her experience, if someone accused of prostitution dared to fight their charges and resist the criminal legal system, police would go out of their way to make their lives a living hell. In her words,

> they try anything in their power to take down this person because this person stood up for themselves. It can even go to harassing the person, like physically assaulting the person.

Not only could someone experience legal retaliation for fighting criminal charges, but they could also be at risk for publicly advocating for sex worker rights. Kim recalls a story about a friend of hers, Gianna, a Black, trans sex worker and activist for sex worker rights, who attended an action in 2013 where she spoke publicly against a predatory diversion program that worked in tandem with law enforcement to arrest sex workers. Later that same night, after the rally, Kim received a call from Gianna who told her she had just been arrested and placed in the very program which they were just protesting.

According to Kim, whenever a sex worker speaks out against police injustices, they would "become a daily target by the police." This not only places them at increased risk for harassment and abuse, but also means that they can "no longer make an income and they have to leave the area." The tactic of cutting off their source of income in order to starve them out of an area is related to the policing of Black, trans sex workers is intended to exclude them from public spaces rather than promote public safety. By making certain spaces uninhabitable for them, the police can effectively silence dissent against the criminal legal system. In other words, driving Black, trans sex workers from public spaces simultaneously reinforces White heteronormativity and police authority.

Not only did participants have to withstand unfounded and fraudulent accusations from police, but they also faced harsher treatment from the criminal legal system than their White and/or cisgender counterparts. Grace speaks of an experience with a White woman she met when first getting into sex work who warned her about such treatment. She says,

> she kind of taught me the ropes and one of the things that I will never forget her telling you was she said, 'you know, one thing about it is that you being a Black, trans girl is you will go to jail doing this, you will spend more time in jail than any of the other girls out here, and you will be harassed more.' And all three of those things came to light and just became truth. On so many occasions I remember thinking back to her telling me that as I was getting arrested, as I was getting assaulted, as I was spending time in jail, remembering this White woman telling me, 'because of who you are this is what's gonna happen,' you know, and she couldn't have been more right.

The consensus among all four respondents is that Black sex workers are stopped by police far more often than White sex workers. In Grace's experience, this divide occurred between Black and non-White people of color, as well as across gender lines. She grew up around mostly White women and can't recall "very many times that [she] ever saw them arrested, saw them harassed."

Similarly, Violet states,

> I compared stories with quite a few White, trans sex workers.... they normally be saying that they rarely don't get targeted. Like they don't really have too much to worry about. But when it came down to, you know, the Black, trans sex workers, it was always a target. It was always - we had to look out. We had to be careful. We had to sneak and do this. We had to... and you know, when the white trans sex workers told me that they don't feel pressured to not do it, they feel okay. They feel comfortable.

In comparison to Black sex workers, White sex workers in Violet's area expressed feeling relatively unworried about coming into contact with the criminal legal system. Being less likely to be stopped by the police means that White sex workers are less likely than their Black counterparts to face violent victimization from law enforcement and the negative effects of becoming involved with the criminal legal system.

In both Violet and Faith's experiences, the racial divide in the number of stops and arrests that trans sex workers have to put up with is, in part, geographically determined. These racial divides along geographic demarcations stem from a long history of segregation. Through processes such as redlining, regional racial divides have become commonplace in the U.S., with members of a given racial or ethnic group tending to live proximal to other members of that same group. These patterns, as my respondents' testimonies show, pervade into subcultures within those communities, thereby affecting, for example, what areas in which a person is likely conduct sex work. In Violet's area, the White sex workers worked in predominantly White neighborhoods while the Black sex workers occupied predominantly Black neighborhoods. Faith's city held several different boroughs, each containing a distinct racial makeup. The districts containing predominantly non-White populations experienced higher rates of policing than the White areas, meaning Black sex workers there had more encounters with law enforcement than their White counterparts.

Not only are Black sex workers policed more, but when White sex workers do encounter law enforcement, officers treat them noticeably better. For example, Olivia's experience, detailed in the previous section, where officers would address her White, trans friends with concern for their safety, and yet would address Olivia with disdain and accusatory questions, exemplifies this pattern. Occasionally, Olivia would leverage the privilege of her White friends and spend more time around them so that the police would overlook her. Such a solution did not last long, however, as the White, trans women would begin to experience more negative encounters with police thanks to their proximity to Black, trans women, like Olivia. In these instances, officers would accuse her of being a bad influence on her friends and "leading [them] down a bad path."

Another difference Olivia notes was whether or not officers thought there was a pimp involved. Officers in her city believed that White sex worker's pimps would keep close watch over them, and thus be nearby if the woman was on the street, as opposed to Black sex worker's pimps who supposedly did not keep such close watch. If a White woman was seen doing sex work without an apparent pimp nearby, officers would assume that she didn't have a pimp. Meanwhile, if a Black woman was working the street with no pimp in sight, officers would follow and harass them to reveal the identity and location of their pimp. This assumption was made by officers regardless of whether the women had pimps or not. Officers additionally assume that if a Black woman is doing sex work alone, that means she is rebelling against her pimp to try and "do her own thing." Olivia points out that this stems from the stereotypes of Black women as angry and standoffish, which in turn derive from the common stereotype of Black people as more aggressive than others (Davis, 1983). Those stereotypes that position Black women as rebellious and ungovernable, thus warranting their policing, are the same ones that denote them as existing outside hegemonic norms of femininity and womanhood (hooks, 2014 and Snorton, 2017). That is to say, stereotypes of Black femininity not only exclude Black, trans women, such as Olivia, from normative ideas of womanhood, but also make them more likely to be policed and punished for their perceived deviance from those racialized gender norms.

To further emphasize the gap in quality of treatment by officers, Grace notes that while "lighter skinned girls" in her area would frequently be taken out on "dates" by police, the officers would coerce and violently force Black sex workers into performing sexual acts on them. This demonstrates that colorism, prejudice against individuals with darker skin tones, is at play in the policing of the sex trade. Lighter skin tones, according to hegemonic standards, denote a proximity to whiteness, and therefore a proximity to social acceptability. In other words, police not only show preference to White sex workers, but also to sex workers within marginalized racial groups who have lighter complexion.

In terms of gender differences, respondents hold that cisgender sex workers almost always received better treatment that trans sex workers because the former are seen as more socially "acceptable" than the latter. Grace elaborates,

> cis women were almost… it's so weird to say this now, but it was almost like they worked with the police, like they always had more of an upper hand with the police than we ever did. You know, like the police officer would stop and talk to the cis girls, you know, in the car and they'd be kikiki-in' and hahaha-in', and buying sodas for them, and checking on them.

Faith notes that cis sex workers would occasionally even have officers as clients - something that was almost never the case for trans sex workers around them. She says, "I knew girls, you know, growing up that police officers was their dates, police officers was their jobs, you know. So, that's not likely to happen for the transgender community."

This is not to say that White and cisgender sex workers never experience any abuse by police (there is no shortage of evidence to the contrary); however, in the respondent's experiences, there was a noticeable difference in patterns of treatment of Black, trans sex workers and White and/or cis sex workers, including the rate and likelihood of arrests. For example, one of Grace's experiences is telling, during which a White, cisgender friend of hers was let go during a sting operation, while Grace was arrested. As she recounts, the police in her area had set up an operation where they would request someone's services online, ask to meet at a hotel, then arrest the person for prostitution when they arrived at the designated hotel room. Her friend, Kate, received a call from what appeared to be a prospective client who asked to meet at a specific hotel room. When she arrived, the man inside admitted to changing his mind and said he was no longer interested, so she left. Later that same day, Grace also received a call from someone asking her to meet at a hotel. Upon exchanging information with her friend, she discovered that it was the exact same hotel room. Assuming he was a client who was only interested in trans women, Grace decided to meet him. They conversed when she arrived, but when they began to negotiate prices, several officers entered the room and arrested her for prostitution. Kate bonded her out of jail and, after corroborating their stories, Grace discovered that the man she met was the same undercover agent who had also met with her friend. The two realized that the man had decided to let Kate go and arrest Grace instead for reasons Grace is confident were based on her race and gender.

Violet advises that there is also a difference in terms of the harshness of punishments with regards to race. According to her, White sex workers often get a "slap on the wrist" compared to the harsher punishments typically faced by Black sex workers. Grace likewise states that "Black cis women were treated harsher, of course, than the cis, White girls," noting that punishments for Black women became even more severe if they were trans. She points out how, when her and other sex workers would be arrested at the same time or around the same area, her White counterparts would be released the next day while she would be made to spend several weeks in jail. Grace's experience of disproportionate jail-time follows a pattern experienced by other Black, trans sex workers. Fitzgerald et al. (2015) demonstrates that Black, trans sex workers typically spend significantly more time in incarceration than their non-Black, non-sex worker counterparts.

Abuse

The final category of direct violence perpetrated by the criminal legal system that the respondents report is abuse. The participants in my study withstood various forms of abuse from agents of the system (almost always police officers). The primary forms of abuse discussed here include verbal abuse, physical abuse, and sexual abuse. Verbal abuse consists of slurs and insults thrown at the women, as well as intentional misgendering of trans subjects by law enforcement officers. Physical abuse typically involves the rough handling of detainees or arrestees by police. Although rare, respondents do recite some instances of extreme police brutality in their communities resulting in the deaths of sex workers. Sexual abuse was the most frequently mentioned form of abuse in conversations with respondents and included solicitation of sex, sexual harassment, sexual assault, and rape by on-duty officers.

Despite police brutality and physical abuse by police being a widespread concern in the U.S., respondents for this study reported that physical violence, such as beatings or killings by officers, were not very common for sex workers, at least not when compared to other forms of abuse. The examples my study's respondents give are mostly second-hand experiences from other sex workers. Grace, for example, when explaining why she stuck primarily to Black neighborhoods in her work, tells how one of her friends, another Black, trans sex worker, was working in a White neighborhood when she was shot by an officer. She was leaving a client's vehicle when the officer approached her. He didn't say anything to her, but when he saw her rummaging in her purse, he reacted by pulling out his gun and shooting her three times in the chest. He later gave the excuse that he assumed she was reaching for a weapon. According to Grace, he remains an active-duty officer in that same county. It does not escape Grace that claiming to fear for their lives because of a suspected, yet unseen, weapon, while tenuous at best, is a common justification used by law enforcement when committing violence against Black people. Her friend's story, as well as more high-profile cases, such as those of Tamir Rice, Jor'Dell Richardson, and Aderrien Murry, demonstrate this and the power of police paranoia in justifying the endangerment of Black lives (Cacho, 2012).

Faith recalls another second-hand story in which a woman of color who worked as a sex worker out of a massage parlor was killed by police violence. Her business was being constantly raided by police officers who would seize her possessions or pressure her into granting them sexual favors. According to Faith, she was reported dead after one of the raids and the officers stated she had leapt from the roof of her building; however, the woman's loved ones and many in her community firmly believe that the officers caused her death as she showed no signs of wanting to take her life prior.

Rather than dismissing these stories off-hand as gossip, it is important to acknowledge the utility of second-hand stories such as these and the integral role they play in marginalized communities and activist circles. As established in previous chapters, the stories of sex workers, particularly those of trans sex workers of color, are often silenced by apathetic news sources, violent retaliation for speaking out against injustice, law enforcement agents sweeping cases under the rug to avoid backlash, or some combination of the three. As is the case with various other marginalized groups, the sex working community maintains knowledge of itself through the circulation of stories that detail their history, their oppression, and their accomplishments. By maintaining this epistemology, the community is able to forge solidarity between its members, since they hold extensive knowledge of their collective oppression, as well as communicate the knowledge to others in order to effect social change. It is common in the Movement for Black Lives, for example, for members to constantly recite the names of forebearers and Black victims of police brutality (i.e., Elijah McClain, Trayvon Martin, Eric Garner, Breonna Taylor). The trans community and sex working community often do the same, reciting the names of individuals, such as Nex Benedict and Marcia Powell, who were killed by bigotry. In doing so, their names simultaneously come to be widely known and recited outside the movement, and to symbolize the struggle for liberation. In other words, the recitation of stories of struggle and the names of people involved works to build power and momentum for a movement. Being such a small percentage of the overall population, it is crucial for sex workers, especially Black, trans sex workers, to keep their stories alive by reciting them within and between communities in order to build momentum within the movement for sex worker rights. As such, the stories recited by Faith and Grace should be considered with due acknowledgment of their validity and significance.

Aside from these extreme examples, the respondents occasionally made brief remarks about how police officers would handle sex workers roughly when arresting them. Violet explains that some of the trans women working the street would have officers "grab them, slam them on a car, make them snatch off their wig, all kinds of crazy disrespectful stuff." Rough treatment such as this seemed to be so commonplace that it was overshadowed by other, more notable instances of abuse. Furthermore, as stated previously, more severe instances of physical abuse by law enforcement are relatively uncommon for sex workers when compared to other forms of abuse.

More common than the physical abuse respondents faced, though often less severe, was verbal abuse. Violet had officers yell at her while they were conducting move-alongs, as did Grace. In some instances, the verbal abuse would escalate to the point where officers were shouting slurs at trans sex workers on the street. Grace recalls experiences with a particularly cruel officer who would shout over his PA system:

> There was this one guy who was just disgusting and he would say stuff like, "do y'all see these trannies out here giving you AIDS?" And "if I catch you picking up one of these trannies, I'm taking you to jail and calling your wife." And like, it was just nasty. I had a cop do that a couple of times.

In such instances, officers would pelt sex workers with slurs, recite harmful stereotypes, and threaten any potential clients as a way of forcing them out of the area. As discussed earlier, intentional misgendering by police is a form of verbal abuse. Officers interacting with Grace when she was doing sex work would constantly address her as "sir" and put unnecessary emphasis on the word. Some would use their PA systems to further emphasize their abuse, saying, "'sir, *sir*, that dress is a little too short, sir. Sir, that hair isn't good on you, sir.'" These types of interactions are intended to degrade trans people, invalidate their identities, and socially discipline their gender expressions. The refusal to address them in a way consistent with their gender identities represents an admonishment of public displays of non-normative gender formations. The fact that such acts are carried out by individuals in positions of power and authority only further adds to the policing effect such admonishment has on the trans community.

While all respondents detail some form of verbal abuse from agents of the criminal justice system, they were usually overshadowed by another form of violence: sexual abuse. Sexual abuse of sex workers by law enforcement is extremely frequent and is one of the most common types of abuse iterated by this study's respondents. Sexual harassment, solicitation, assault, and rape comprise the various forms of sexual abuse committed by agents of the criminal legal system. Officers frequently sexually harass sex workers, especially Black, trans sex workers, through processes of degradation that include misgendering, inappropriate comments, and unnecessary strip searches. Sexual solicitation by officers is extremely common, and almost all of my study's respondents report being subjected to some form of solicitation. Such acts represent egregious abuses of power and are offered by officers in exchange for leniency. Sexual assault and rape by officers are constant threats for sex workers. In such situations, there is no promise of leniency involved, and instead the officers coerce the survivors of assault through threats of arrest or further violence.

The respondents detail myriad experiences of sexual harassment. Violet's recollection of unnecessary searches where officers would rip off trans women's wigs, clothes, and other items is one such example. Grace's stories of multiple officers referring to her and other Black, trans sex workers with slurs and other derogatory, sexual terms offer further insight into the forms of sexual harassment Black, trans sex workers experience when working the streets. Notably, the testimonies of my study's respondents show that Black, trans individuals are at risk of sexual abuse from police regardless of whether they were participating in sex work at the time. For example, Grace recalls that despite identifying and presenting as women while incarcerated, she and her friends were placed in the male pods. The placement of trans people in sections of jails or prisons that do not align with their gender identity is a common practice that often endangers the incarcerated individual (Grant et al., 2011 and Ritchie, 2013). Police departments across the country report either having no policy in place for the placement of trans inmates, or determining placement according to an inmate's genitalia, meaning many trans women get placed in the men's pods and vice-versa (Amnesty International, 2005). When trans women are placed in male pods, officers in these pods will occasionally conduct invasive strip searches on the women in full view of the other inmates. Grace's description of being unreasonably strip searched in jail is illustrative. The correctional officer in those instances would intentionally conduct the searches in full view of the other inmates in the male pod as a way of sexually humiliating her and other trans women. The thinly veiled pretense one officer used was that the women were regularly leaving the jail to do community service and thus had to be searched to ensure no contraband had been smuggled in. Sometimes, he would conduct these searches on the trans women in the jail even if they hadn't gone out for community service that day, supporting Grace's suspicion that the harassment was due to transphobic discrimination.

Faith recalls a story of sexual harassment by officers which took place during her childhood. When she was about ten years old, she had her first encounter with the police. She was out late, around midnight, and was rushing home; however, the path she had to take was through a section of the city known for drug dealing and prostitution, and so had a high rate of policing. While in this section of the city, Faith was stopped by a couple officers who assumed she was selling drugs. She tried explaining that she was just a kid, but the police proceeded to search her and ordered her to pull her pants down, at which point they saw she was wearing tight fitting Adidas shorts underneath. Faith explains that by this point in her childhood, she had already realized she was trans, and hence wore some clothing items considered traditionally feminine. The officers derided her for her clothing, telling her to "pull [her] panties up." After seeing her school ID during the stop, the officers, rather than expressing concern or offering to get her home safely, called out to some presumed drug dealers on the corner of the street and yelled, "[L]ook at this faggot over here in red shorts!" before driving off and leaving Faith vulnerable. Thankfully, the people on the corner were unbothered, so no harm befell her. It was obvious to Faith, however, that the officers' intentions were to put her in a dangerous situation where she could be harassed, assaulted, or worse, all because she dared to defy gender norms.

In addition to sexual harassment, Black, trans sex workers are often propositioned by officers for sexual favors in exchange for leniency. Olivia voices experiences where she would be propositioned in such a way when she was conducting sex work as a minor. At the time, she was willing to humor the officers if it meant she wouldn't see a jail cell that night. However, afterwards, she remembers the advances as unwanted and exploitative. According to her, the officers "[knew] they [could] do it because [she was] already in the act." In such instances where officers make sexual advances on civilians, the victim may not feel like they have a choice in the matter due to the uneven power dynamic. Thus, even if the officer isn't overtly coercive, the citizen lacks the ability to fully consent to sexual acts with the former. This type of interaction is referred to as "quid-pro-quo" and is prevalent in police departments across the nation (Stinson et al., 2015). Furthermore, it is found to be disproportionately used against sex workers and other vulnerable groups that officers deem "less credible" (Borchetta & Morris, 2023 and Stinson et al., 2020).

Other times, officers offer Black, trans women leniency in exchange for sex, but still arrest them soon after. Grace recounts one such experience where she knew an officer who promised to make sure she wouldn't be arrested by other officers in exchange for sex. After one exchange, the officer returned with a few other officers just a couple days later to harass Grace and her friends for sexual favors. When the abuse of power became too much for Grace, she "cut them off," after which the officers retaliated by arresting her. Those officers would sometimes even go so far as to falsify reports to stack more charges against her.

In other instances of sexual abuse by police, officers would be more forceful in their exploitation, opting to aggressively coerce the women with threats of violence or arrest. According to respondents, this form of aggressive coercion was more often experienced by Black sex workers, while their White counterparts more often experienced coercion in the form of officers propositioning them for "dates" for which they would sometimes even pay the White sex workers. Although both instances of coercion constitute acts of sexual assault/rape, participants perceived the coercion of Black sex workers to be noticeably more violent. Grace describes the difference in treatment between Black and non-Black sex workers, explaining that,

> most of the time, the lighter-skinned girls would get invited on dates by them. "Oh, well, when I'm off duty, I'd love to take you out. I'd love for you to come over and hang out. I'd love for you to..." And the Black girls were like, "get the fuck in the back seat of the car, come do what the fuck I want you to do, and then I'm going to drop you off and you better never tell anyone about it."

This demonstrates influences of colorism and racism in the course of officer sexual misconduct, whereby White and "lighter-skinned" sex workers receive better treatment than their darker-skinned, Black counterparts. Moreover, it shows the effect of prior discussed racist stereotypes that reduce Black bodies to sexuality (Davis, 1986; hooks, 2014; and Mercer, 1994). While White sex workers are more often treated as people, Black sex workers are disregarded as deserving of such respect because their sexuality, in the officers' eyes, takes precedence over their personhood.

In another instance, Grace was caught by an officer with one of her clients and coerced into sex. She explains,

> he told the guy to step away for a moment. When the guy stepped away, he said, "this is what's going to happen. You're going to finish this guy up and get him out of here. And then you're going to do me or you're both going to jail." And I'm like, well, that's not really an option. You know what I mean?… That's not a question. Like, so, of course, I did what I had to do. But yeah, that kind of stuff happens all the time.

Coercing sex from sex workers under threat of arrest is an egregious abuse of power and constitutes rape due to the lack of consent concerning power differentials. It should be noted that in some areas, such as Violet's city, cisgender sex workers were more likely than trans sex workers to be sexually exploited by officers in that way. Her area was predominantly Black, so the population she primarily saw experiencing this form of abuse was comprised mostly of Black, cis women. According to Violet, officers would abuse their power to proposition sex workers in as much as half of police stops and confrontations. Faith claims that trans women of color were targeted particularly often by officers who abused their power to commit rape. She indicates a problematic pattern in a region whose racial makeup consisted of mostly Black and Latine folk, where the sex workers were typically Black or Latina trans women. In that region of the city, Faith noted that undercover officers would frequently coerce the women into performing sexual acts on them under threat of arrest. Oftentimes, however, the officers would arrest the women after the sexual act anyways, which she indicated left the women "feeling like they [had] just been degraded and raped."

In some circumstances, police would be even more forceful and violent when demanding sexual favors from sex workers. Respondents report multiple instances of what can only be described as extra-judicial kidnappings by police officers, during which they would rape the sex worker they kidnapped and threaten the survivors with arrest or violence if they dared to report the assault. Though she was fortunate enough to not experience this, Violet states that there were multiple instances that have occurred where a trans sex worker "thought they were going to be arrested, took somewhere and by the police, been taken advantage of and let go. And were told not to say anything or they're going to jail." Grace described this happening, not to her, but to another Black, trans sex worker she worked alongside.

She explains that,

> there was this one officer who used to do it to her almost once a week, like to the point where she would try to hide from him when it was that day and she knew he was going to be on shift that night because he was going to kidnap her basically in the backseat of the car, you know, like throw her in the backseat car, put cuffs on her in the whole nine yards like she was being arrested, but he would take her somewhere, he would do whatever he wanted with her, make her do whatever he wanted, and then he would drop her off way away from wherever we were and make her walk back to us. And he used to do that to her on a regular basis.

Kim corroborates such claims and explains that in her experience as an activist for sex worker rights, the police in her city believed that sex workers existed to "gratify them sexually." According to her, the kidnapping and rape of both cis and trans women by police was frequent in her area. She saw this as an issue across racial and gender lines, such that anyone who was a sex worker, or "stigmatized as such," was at risk for this form of abuse.

Research further supports the claims and shows police officers disproportionately commit rape against Black people, trans people, and sex workers. Stinson et al. (2020) found that involvement in the sex industry was one of the largest predictors of victimization regarding police sexual violence, and that, of the cases successfully reported by sex workers, nearly half involved forcible rape. Fitzgerald et al. (2015) also looked at the effect of involvement in the sex trade on sexual victimization rates and found that trans sex workers were nearly three times more likely than trans non-sex workers to be raped by officers and prison staff (10.7% versus 3.8%). Amnesty International (2005) and Ritchie (2013) documented several instances of rape by officers and detention facility staff reported by Black and trans survivors. Further, Grant et al. (2011) found that trans people, particularly trans women, faced significant rates of sexual assault by jail and prison staff (7%), and that Black, trans individuals in incarceration were more likely than almost every other racial group to be sexually assaulted by staff (9%).

While some might believe the obvious solution to these issues would be to report the crimes being committed by police officers, this can prove dangerous for Black, trans folk because it carries the risk of retaliation. Amnesty International (2005) points out that officer misconduct goes under-reported partially due to fear of retaliation. By reporting sexual misconduct by police, survivors run the risk of being further harassed and abused by law enforcement agents, therefore increasing their chances of victimization, and resulting in loss of income. Even when retaliation is not a concern, however, those who wish to report sexual violence at the hands of police officers typically encounter the "blue wall of silence," the unofficial code of silence that discourages officers from reporting misconduct by their colleagues (Stinson et al., 2020). This usually manifests in the almost immediate discreditation of the survivor's claims of victimization, either through disparagement of the survivor's character or the refusal to investigate issues without "sufficient" evidence (Amnesty International, 2005). As Amnesty International notes, police perpetrators of sexual violence often act with impunity thanks to institutionalized discrimination against queer and trans populations as hypersexual, deviant, and less credible.

Violet explains that when it comes to reporting officers for sexual violence, it is "your reputation against the officer's reputation." She elaborates, explaining that "they figure you're a sex worker, you out here doing this, you probably wanted it, or you probably forced yourself on the officer or so forth or whatever." Social norms surrounding sexuality dictate that a sexual violence survivor's status as a sex worker essentially revokes one's status as a "proper" victim. Grace states that even if the police did write up some kind of report on officer misconduct, the report itself was often dismissive and blamed the victim. She says,

> it basically was spun, like, "oh, a black tranny with a drug history" - mind you, the drug history was marijuana - "Black tranny with a drug history accuses upstanding officer of rape...." So, it was always spinned [sic] where we blame the victim, and the officer looks like the poor guy who's being accused by these - these trannies.

In Grace's retelling of her experiences, officers placed emphasis on the fact that the reporting party was transgender. Gender obviously plays a notable role in these interactions, with Violet explaining that officers will sometimes blame the survivor for their assault by pointing out that they "probably didn't tell [the attacker] that [they] were trans." This is a clear manifestation of the stereotype of trans people (particularly trans women) as sexual deviants whose aim is to trick "innocent" straight men into having sex with them.

Researchers have documented several instances in which violence against trans people has been justified by the belief that victims sought to deceive heterosexual people into intimacy (Amnesty International, 2005 and Stryker, 2006). Schilt & Westbrook (2009), Sloop (2000), and MacKenzie & Marcel (2009) all point out that such perceptions of trans people are emphasized by negative media portrayals of them as deceitful. These beliefs are ultimately rooted in hegemonic constructions of gender as intrinsically linked to biological sex. Because gender is linked to sex, and thus viewed as immutable, trans identities, which fall outside the normative idea of gender, are viewed as conscious choices (Stryker, 2006). Furthermore, hegemonic culture places great emphasis on the reproductive nature of biological sex. Such emphasis carries the effect of sexualizing the notion of gender, therefore surmising that one expresses gender in order to attract one's desired sexual partner (Butler, 1988, 2006). Trans people are thus seen as choosing to flout gender norms in order to attract members of the same sex/gender and participate in "unnatural" homo-erotic sex (Anzani et al., 2021). As sexually deviant "tricksters," trans survivors of sexual violence are seen as deserving of the acts perpetrated against them and are considered unworthy of protection.

As this chapter has demonstrated, Black, trans sex workers are subject to myriad forms of violence and abuse carried out by agents of the criminal legal system. This study's respondents and various historical narratives indicate that harassment, false accusations, unnecessarily harsh treatment, verbal abuse, physical abuse, and sexual abuse comprise the primary forms of violence that Black, trans sex workers experience from law enforcement and others within the criminal legal system. Harassment detailed in this study primarily includes move-alongs, derogatory insults, misgendering, unnecessary searches, and racist, transphobic surveillance practices. All forms of harassment are reported to be disproportionately leveraged against Black, trans, and low-income people in the sex working community. Black, trans people also face fraudulent, unfounded allegations of prostitution and harsher than normal punishments at higher rates than their White and cisgender counterparts. Furthermore, this study demonstrates that agents of the criminal legal system disproportionately commit acts of verbal, physical, and sexual abuse against Black, trans sex workers.

These patterns of violence detailed in this chapter illustrate a relationship between the criminal legal system and Black, trans sex workers in which the former exercises disciplinary power to forward biopolitical goals of the state. By enacting violence on Black, trans sex workers and those stigmatized as such, the criminal legal system maintains their position at the bottom of hegemonic hierarchies while reinforcing White, cis-heteropatriarchal dominance. While this chapter illustrated the forms of *direct* violence perpetrated by agents of the criminal legal system, the following chapter details the ways in which the system *indirectly* contributes to the harm and violence faced by Black, trans individuals. Most often, indirect violence perpetrated by the system involves its agents either intentionally or unintentionally placing the subjects in situations in which they are increasingly likely to be victimized by others.

CHAPTER IV

INDIRECT VIOLENCE PERPETRATED BY THE CRIMINAL LEGAL SYSTEM

There are multiple ways in which the criminal legal system indirectly inflicts violence upon Black, trans sex workers. These primarily include the use of sex work diversion programs, placing Black, trans people in men's jails, and rendering Black, trans sex workers unable to rely on law enforcement in times of crisis. Sex work diversion programs tend not only to violate participants' rights by working separately from the police and courts, but also turn the focus from systemic issues to individual sex workers. When incarcerated with men, sex workers, especially Black, trans ones, face extremely high risks of violent victimization at the hands of correctional staff and other inmates. Finally, by neglecting to help them when they are the victims of crimes, law enforcement places the lives of Black, trans workers in jeopardy as their neglect signals to others that they can inflict violence upon the sex workers with impunity. All of these forms of violence reinforce the oppression of Black, trans sex worker and uphold the dominance of White, cis-heteropatriarchal society.

Men's Pods & Diversion Programs

Being placed in men's pods when incarcerated is one form of indirect police-inflicted harm mentioned by my respondents. Being in these pods places trans individuals at great risk of experiencing sexual assault, rape, and physical violence from fellow inmates, with, as James et al. (2016) found, 16% of incarcerated trans individuals experiencing physical assault from other inmates. The rates of such experiences are startlingly high for trans individuals as James et al. estimate that trans individuals are nine to ten times more likely (17%) than the general incarcerated population to be sexually assaulted by another inmate. As these numbers make clear, research shows that trans folk are at high risk of experiencing violence and harassment during incarceration. Black, trans sex workers are at even greater risk for sexual assault. Grant et al. (2011) found that Black, trans inmates were at higher risk of being assaulted by other inmates when compared to their non-Black counterparts. Incarcerated Black, trans individuals experienced the highest rate of sexual assault from other inmates (32%) and the second highest rate of physical assault from other inmates (29%), second only to Native American, trans individuals who experienced a rate of 42%. On the other hand, White, trans subjects experienced the lowest rate of physical assault (9%) and the second lowest rate of (7%). Moreover, Fitzgerald et al. (2015) found that the likelihood of being harassed or assaulted by other inmates was significantly higher for sex workers than non-sex workers. Incarcerated sex workers were more likely to be harassed, physically assaulted, and sexually assaulted (52.6%, 13.5%, and 10.7%, respectively) compared to their non-sex worker counterparts (28.9%, 5.3%, and 3.8%, respectively). This startlingly high rates of victimization for trans people, Black trans people especially, and sex workers are the reason that groups such as Amnesty International (2005) highly recommend that correctional facilities revise their policies and prioritize safety for trans individuals by avoiding placing them in clearly dangerous environments, such as men's pods. These statistics clearly communicate that Black, trans sex workers who are incarcerated with male inmates are in intense danger. Well aware of the danger and the likelihood of being harmed in men's jails, my participants expressed fears associated with being incarcerated with male inmates, as well as experiences of harassment and assault of them and their peers.

Despite clearly being in danger, Grace reports that she and other Black, trans sex workers in her area were always placed in men's cells when incarcerated. Being placed in a men's cell was a constant fear for Grace. Many Black, trans sex workers around her were beaten up and raped by other inmates when they were sent to jail. She recites one such story, stating,

> one of them was a postdoc, actually. And she tried to tell them that, "if you throw me into a men's cell, like it's going to be hell." And I think that they did it purposely, kind of like an experiment to see what would happen. And sure enough, she wasn't there maybe six hours and she got raped, gang raped.

Grace expresses being extraordinarily lucky in her experiences of being incarcerated. She went out of her way to avoid other inmates and fly under the radar during her time in jail, resulting in her fortunately escaping assault by other inmates. Curiously enough, Grace reveals that the inmates she did interact with seemed to "cling" to her and were somewhat "protective" over her. In fact, the only assault or harassment she experienced while incarcerated came at the hands of correctional officers. However fortuitous and ostensibly unexpected it might be, Grace's story follows a pattern reflected by research into the imprisonment of trans individuals. Research has shown that incarcerated trans individuals are typically more likely to experience harassment or assault from correctional facility staff than other inmates (Fitzgerald et al., 2015; Grant et al., 2011; and James et al., 2016). In other words, the facility staff charged with the safety of the inmates are a greater danger to incarcerated trans people than other inmates. Men's pods in jail are not the only harmful contexts in which police place Black, trans sex workers. Diversion programs, though they don't carry nearly the same risks for physical or sexual assault, present their own unique forms of harm.

Some within the sex trade find that diversion programs meant to deter people from entering the sex trade present another form of indirect harm from the criminal legal system. For example, Project ROSE, an "anti-trafficking" initiative in Arizona, was widely determined by sex workers and their advocates to be coercive and biased toward marginalized groups including people of color, queer folk, and those living in poverty (Strangio, 2014). The Phoenix police would conduct mass sting operations administered through Project ROSE that resulted in hundreds of arrests of individuals suspected of prostitution (Grant, 2014). Rather than being taken to the police department and given proper counsel, those arrested in the stings were taken to churches where they would be compelled to answer questions about their involvement in the sex trade during interviews. These interviews would be conducted without legal counsel present and would be used against the defendants in court if they did not qualify for the program ("Project ROSE Ends", 2014).

While ostensibly intended to combat sex-trafficking, diversion programs like project ROSE "[infringe] on protected free speech rights and [prohibit] conduct that expresses gender identity" ("Project ROSE ends", 2014). Furthermore, they violate individuals' due process rights as they are not afforded proper counsel. Still, the criminal legal system insists that these programs are helpful and voluntary, but as Kim states in her interview with me,

> Nobody voluntarily gets taken off the street, handcuffed, placed in the back of a police car, and driven not to a court of law or a system of government, but to a church.

Kim's statement emphasizes the subtly insidious nature of the operation of some diversion programs. Taking detainees to a church instead of a court and placing them before a non-profit worker rather than an officer prevents them from accessing certain rights, such as the right to counsel, therefore coercing them into complying with the program as they are given little choice otherwise.

The respondents of this study have mixed views on diversion programs, their effectiveness, and the potential harm they inflicted to participants. Olivia, for example, explains that her experience was more akin to "sexual therapy" than anything else. During her time in the sex work diversion program in her area, she was continuously asked questions such as "why are you promiscuous? Do you think that not having a parent leads to your promiscuity?" Such questions come off as accusatory, as though the interviewer is approaching the other person with the intent of shaming their sexuality. Questions pertaining to the interviewees' lack of family support feel particularly pointed considering the fact that many trans youths are kicked out of their homes or disowned due to their gender identities. Olivia explains that the experience "felt like a study project", where she was a subject to be studied rather than an individual with autonomy, agency, and intelligence. This form of "aid" given to sex workers, particularly trans women in sex work, reinforces hegemonic norms of sexuality as it attempts to shame them for their deviant sexuality. Olivia's experience also illuminates neoliberal approaches to social issues within diversion programs which make hyperindividualistic assumptions that find fault with an individual's morality rather than potential flaws in the institutions surrounding them (Davis et al., 2022). In this way, rather than addressing the circumstances that placed Olivia in the position of needing to do sex work, diversion programs would rather examine her character and the presumed flaws therein.

Faith's experience regarding diversion programs differed. She was never directly involved in any of the programs herself, but knew other Black, trans individuals who were. She was told by others involved in the programs that they did not have good experiences. Faith also spoke with someone who worked in the program, and the conclusion she drew from her conversation with them was that those who had negative views were "just being lazy and not wanting to do" the work that was required of them. She expresses that, while she understood the demands of the program could be difficult to meet, participants should focus on the "bigger picture", which was that they were able to stay out of jail because of the program. This diversion program's approach operates similarly to the one Olivia was involved in by offering temporary solutions that focus on the behavior and morality of the individual rather than addressing the root causes of the issues that lead to people needing to rely on sex work. Such approaches to social issues run the risk of aiding in the preservation of regulatory institutions, such as the criminal legal system, because they function to distract from systemic flaws and instead draw attention to the individual. The sex work diversion program in Faith's city was specifically geared toward Black and trans folk involved in the sex trade. In the area where Grace conducted sex work, diversion programs had no such intent, and while she was never involved with such organizations herself, she notes that Black, trans women were often denied the option entirely. In her former city, the goal of law enforcement was to "keep [trans women] locked up" and off the street. In other words, the criminal legal system had no intent of aiding Black, trans folk through available social systems, preferring instead to criminalize them as though ridding the city of an infection.

Violet herself worked in a diversion program in her city and doesn't have much of anything negative to say about her experiences, saying instead, "It was basically a get out of jail free card." The program she worked with was geared toward trans folk and her job was to work with the judge to enroll them in the project and drop their charges if they successfully completed its requirements. She does mention that, like with Project ROSE, many trans individuals were arrested and essentially coerced into undergoing the program despite not having participated in sex work when they were arrested. In her eyes, however, the diversion program in her area was useful in that it provided a way for innocent people to avoid unnecessary jail time. Once again, this perspective shifts the focus from the institution to the individual as the source of social issues. On a micro-scale, as Faith and Violet explain, these programs do have some practical utility for those involved as they offer participants a way to avoid immediate negative consequences, such as incarceration. However, when viewed at a societal level, such approaches to social issues reinforce hegemonic views on race, gender, class, and sexuality because the focus on the flaws of the individuals also places their non-normative identities at the forefront of the discussion, thus framing their deviance from societal norms as part of the problem.

Inability to Rely on Law Enforcement

The most pervasive form of indirect violence from the criminal legal system stemmed from the fact that the respondents were unable to rely on the system when in danger. Specifically, respondents explain that they and other Black, trans sex workers were unable to receive adequate assistance from law enforcement. Officers would often refuse to file reports and would discredit the victim by accusing them of wrongdoing or otherwise try to dissuade the victim from filing a report.

Violet illustrates the accusatory nature of interactions she and others would have with police when calling to report a crime against them:

> the complaints go nowhere. They feel like for one, you probably didn't tell them that you were trans. Two, because you're out here having sex with these people. Three, you probably on drugs. Four, because you out here and you liked it and he probably didn't give you enough money and that's probably why you making a complaint….

As Violet explains, the women's identities as both trans and sex workers played a significant factor in the police refusing to acknowledge their victimization. Grace and Olivia both report similar experiences, stating that the police would blame them for being assaulted. Grace finds it ironic that the people that were ostensibly meant to protect her would instead choose to "victim-blame" her and grill her with accusatory questions. As Olivia explained, officers would ask, "What made him do that to you? What did you say? What did you do?" For Violet, the questions specifically pertained to whether or not she was doing sex work. The officers in their experiences immediately assumed that they had done something to deserve violence from others and were therefore unworthy of protection from law enforcement.

Violet points out that police would take an accusatory stance when addressing Black, trans women regardless of whether they were actually participating in sex work or any illegal activities at the time. While not citing specific questions officers would ask, Faith confirmed that after being robbed, beaten, or raped, sex workers would be demonized and disrespected by police who ultimately didn't care what happened to the girls.

Grace details a particularly poignant story in which a would-be client tried to kill her, and the police offered no help. She rode with a client in his vehicle to a parking lot near a hotel. After he parked the car, he walked out to her side, opened her door, dragged her out, and proceeded to continually beat her across the head. She fought him for several minutes before collapsing from exhaustion, at which point he returned to his car and fled, attempting to run over her head on the way out. Having survived, Grace ran into the hotel and asked a woman working at the front desk to call the police. She was obviously wounded and bleeding profusely, but rather than acting with urgency, the woman she spoke to was hesitant to call the police because of the stigma attached to Grace as a sex worker. She eventually called the police, who arrived thirty minutes later and proceeded to discourage her from filing a report. They convinced her it would be difficult for her to convince a judge or jury of the assault because she would have to inform them why she was with the man in the first place, strongly insinuating that they stigmatized Grace as a sex worker and thus undeserving of justice. She describes how,

> ...I remember having to get on the bus that morning at like five o'clock in the morning with [sic] still bleeding because I had no medical care that was provided to me. Still bleeding and my hair was still in the parking lot. My clothes are still ripped. And I remember having to get on the bus in the tourist area to get back to my neighborhood looking like that and feeling like that, and just remembering the looks and the stares of everybody, and feeling like I have no one that has my back. You know, there is no authority that has my back and that protects me.

In the officers' eyes, Grace's identity as a trans woman stigmatized for sex work denoted her as someone unworthy of protection and safety. As such, she was bereft of the safety net that many others are able to enjoy, the criminal legal system.

Even when they had no involvement in the sex trade, some respondents report trans individuals being denied police assistance due to the sexualization of their identities. Olivia, for example, explains how a trans girl in her city was physically assaulted at her high school by another student with whom she'd been intimate. Despite reporting it to the school, authorities refused to do anything about the assault and claimed that she was likely victimized because the other student was new to the school and must not have known she was trans. In the eyes of her school's authorities, the trans girl was deserving of abuse simply because of her gender identity. Just as Grace and other respondents were identified as sexual deviants on account of their involvement in the sex trade, the girl in Olivia's story was labeled such because of her transness, thus depriving her of any protection from violence.

In the examples detailed above, police and other penal authorities go out of their way to avoid offering legal protection by refusing to file reports or deterring victims from doing so. However, even when reports were filed and the officers did not outright deny the victimization of respondents and other Black, trans individuals, reports were not likely to result in any further action. When she was physically assaulted by a would-be client who felt he'd been "tricked", Olivia called the police immediately following the incident. The officers who arrived seemed to express concern at first, but the interaction quickly turned to accusations and victim-blaming. The officers seemed more concerned with what Olivia did to supposedly deserve violence than with her safety. Nonetheless, they took her statement, and she was able to file a report. According to her, however, nothing ever came of it. There was no follow-up or investigation from the police and the man who assaulted her went unpunished. Olivia states that she no longer goes to the police for help when she is in danger.

Olivia's feelings of cynicism toward the reliability of law enforcement are, unfortunately, not unique. Lack of faith in police is pervasive within the sex trade and those in the industry tend to avoid relying on law enforcement if possible. As Violet states regarding the sentiment of the sex working community, "everyone already knew the police wasn't on their side." This lack of confidence in law enforcement is due not only to their frequent neglect of the needs of sex workers, but also to the consistent patterns of violence imposed upon sex workers by officers themselves. As discussed in the previous chapter, harassment, abuse, and other forms of violence perpetrated by police are common in the sex trade. Relying on the police for help therefore only places sex workers at greater risk of being victimized by them because of the resultant interactions between the two.

Study respondents detailed three primary reasons why the inability to rely on police place sex workers at large, and Black, trans sex workers in particular, at increased risk of violence. First, sex workers are at increased risk of experiencing various forms of victimization when compared to non-sex workers; this is especially the case for Black and trans sex workers. Sex workers, therefore, find themselves in need of police assistance more often than many others and are at increased risk of danger since the criminal legal system has proved unreliable to them.

Second, it is widely known that police are less likely to help sex workers than non-sex workers, especially if the sex worker in question is a racial, gender, or sexual minority. As a result, many of those who target sex workers for crimes do so specifically because they know they are likely to get away with it. In other words, sex workers are more likely to be targeted for violence because many of those who target them are aware the police are not likely to help. Third, and finally, because they are unable to seek help from law enforcement, sex workers are often made to find ways of protecting themselves. However, devising methods of self-protection in lieu of the criminal legal system can, ironically, place individuals in the sex trade at increased risk of abuse from officers. Some of the methods sex workers use for self-protection are illegal, are otherwise prohibited, and sometimes lead officers to label certain individuals as dangerous or violent, thus making it more likely that police will confront them and possibly harass/abuse them. This paradoxical situation forces sex workers to choose between appearing less threatening before the police and defending themselves from crime victimization. It is no surprise that many choose the latter, considering the frequency with which they are targeted for crimes such as robbery.

Participants' statements reveal that robbery was the most common crime for which they were targeted by non-law enforcement individuals. Grace states that being robbed was a "regular thing" when she worked the street. Potential clients would express interest and set up appointments, only for them to try and rob her upon meeting. According to her,

> there was one point in time that I was a street girl, so I worked the corners and jumping in and out of cars with complete strangers. So there were many experiences of assault. There were many experiences of robbing, getting robbed.

Faith explains that whenever sex workers are robbed, they are overwhelmingly likely to share the experience with their community and friends rather than police because they feel, at best, they would receive no aid and, at worst, they would be arrested for prostitution. Once a person starts sex work, Olivia says, word spreads and others start to view them as a "high paying trick". As a result, she and other sex workers become more likely to be targeted for robbery than non-sex workers.

Racial and gender stereotypes play a significant part in who was targeted for robbery. According to Olivia, Black, trans women were seen as "exotic" by clients and were thus more sought after. Johns in Violet's area also preferred Black, trans women with dark complexions, specifying that clients would often favor those who were "less passable" or "more masculine". Because they were more sought after (or perceived to be), Black, trans sex workers were more likely to be targeted for robbery because it was assumed they made more money than others.

However, Grace's experience differed, and she reported that cisgender, non-Black, and "passable" trans women were seen as more desirable in the areas she worked. Likewise, "light skinned" non-Black women in Faith's area seemed to be more sought after. Despite being seen as less desirable than their non-Black and cisgender counterparts, however, Black, trans sex workers in Grace and Faith's areas were still more likely to be targeted for crimes involving robbery, violence, and harassment.

Other than robbery, respondents experienced increased risk of other crimes, such as physical assault, rape, and murder. Some examples were already detailed above, such as Olivia being physically assaulted by a john and Grace being nearly killed as a man tried to run her over. Violet expresses that when she started sex work, it quickly became dangerous and trans women around her "were getting robbed, raped, and even murdered." Grace conveys similar fears, stating,

> you fear that you don't know the people that you're meeting up with. You don't know what their intentions are. You don't know if you're gonna make it out of that situation to the next one.

Faith was able to avoid many dangerous interactions with johns by learning from the mistakes of those around and being extremely resourceful with the methods of self-protection available to her at the time. She still holds similar anxieties, citing them as the reasons she went to such great pains to avoid potential danger.

Danger came not only from police, johns, transphobic strangers, but from individuals within the respondents' own communities as well. Violet explains how other trans women around her would express "cattiness" in response to her perceived success in the sex trade, sparking various fights with others where she had to physically defend herself. Such cattiness was also present in Faith's experience, particularly in the ballroom scene, a community in which Black, trans folk are largely present and influential. Citing various reasons (e.g., being more passable, making more money, and having more successful relationships than others), Faith reports that she would experience harassment from others in her community which involved them reporting her to the authorities for sex work, despite the fact they had little to no evidence. This sort of conflict between community members reflects the mechanisms of dominant institutions which function to divide communities by encouraging adherence to social hierarchies. Rather than aiding each other and building each other up as a community, members of Faith's community sought instead to sabotage her to elevate their own statuses in the hierarchy. This was especially harmful to Faith who was passionate about raising kids of her own and was thus fostering children at the time. The reports resulted in CPS becoming involved. In her state, being reported to CPS as a foster parent immediately resulted in the children being taken away, regardless of whether or not the allegations were true. In other words, even though law enforcement was unable to find evidence of her participating in sex work, her foster children were still taken from her several times due to harassment from others in her community.

In some instances, such as those described above, Black, trans folk are targeted specifically because perpetrators know the victims can't rely on police. Those inflicting violence upon sex workers, especially those in other marginalized communities, are therefore seen as safe targets who one can harm with impunity. When speaking about how the police are unreliable for Black, trans sex workers, Grace explains,

> we're not the only ones that know that, Sasha. The dates know that. The clients know that. They know that if I beat this bitch up or if I robbed this bitch, or if I do this, if I do that, they're not, chances are, they're not going to call the cops. You know, the chances are, if they do call the cops, the cops aren't going to buy it. The cops aren't going to believe it.... So, yeah, the clients know that just as much as we do. So, it absolutely does make it a very dangerous experience.

In other words, perpetrators of violence against sex workers, particularly Black, trans sex workers, intentionally target them because they are aware that the criminal legal system will likely do little to aid their victims. Grace has had several clients recite that very sentiment to her: that police would not help her as a sex worker. Clients have asked her, "'if you call the police, who are you going to call? Who are you going to tell? Who's going to believe you? Who's going to listen to you? You know, a prostitute, who's going to listen to you?'" Violet expresses a similar sentiment:

> someone I dated that actually knew someone that was actually out robbing and raping trans women. So yeah, that's exactly what they believe… that when it comes down to, you know, robbing or raping or whatever with trans women, they feel like the police not really going to do too much. And technically the police doesn't do too much because a trans person can go to a police officer and say, "hey, I've been robbed or I've been raped." And the first thing the police gon' say was, "were you tricking or were you doing sex work?" And it goes no further than that.

These statements reveal that the criminal legal system's enmity toward certain marginalized communities operates as a cultural signifier that increases the risk of harm for those groups. The mistreatment of and lack of concern for sex workers by the criminal legal system is so evident that the system indirectly harms the group by designating its members as individuals whom it is acceptable to victimize.

Since they are in so much danger and are unable to rely on law enforcement, sex workers often are inevitably made to find ways of defending themselves in lieu of protection from the state. One of the most common forms of self-protection reported by respondents was close community involvement. Grace stressed how important it was to stick close to your "sisters" who "understand your everyday struggles". She recalled working in an area of her city that was something of a "gay resort" where cisgender, transgender, male, and female alike worked in relatively close proximity. However, Grace acknowledged that there were gaps in understanding regarding the racialized realities of various groups in the sex trade. Growing up around mostly White, trans women, she remarked that they weren't able to fully grasp the struggles she went through on account of her race. For Grace, this meant that she needed to be in close community with other Black, trans women who shared many experiences with her that White, trans women typically did not.

Faith reports that the queer community in her area went out of its way to protect its younger members. As discussed earlier, trans youths are at a higher risk of being kicked out of their homes when compared to their cisgender counterparts. In response, many older individuals in the trans community in Violet's area will take them in and form surrogate families so the youths will have shelters and support systems. The goal in these cases, Violet explained to prevent the youths from having to turn to sex work for survival due to how dangerous it can be, especially for those who are inexperienced. Yet, despite the community efforts in cities such as Violet's, many trans youths still must rely on sex work for survival. In Faith's community, the "elder girls" would go out of their way to supply those of the younger generation with the knowledge needed to keep themselves safe. The women would give tips, such as "get your money up front" and "no glove, no love."

The sex worker community also supported itself by spreading information about dangerous individuals to others who were at risk of being targeted for violence. Word of mouth was the primary method of information distribution in Grace's area when she was a sex worker. When anyone in her community would have a bad experience, they would tell "at least two or three other people" who would then spread the word throughout the community. She recalls one such experience:

> there was a guy I remember in a gold truck, never knew the guy's name. He was a Spanish guy in a gold truck that he used to pick up the girls and like hit them and basically rough sex with them and then like treat them like dirt and trash. And it wasn't, it wasn't part of the experience. It was like this was what got him off was treating girls like shit. And so, so, I remember how quickly it spread the news spread for him. And so, when he would come out, like literally everyone would know and he would be mad because no one would get in his car.

By communicating with each other, Grace's community was able to protect itself from harmful clients. Violet's community did the same through "bad date sheets". When a sex worker was robbed, raped or assaulted, they would give the information to someone who would then compile a list of dangerous individuals, their physical description, their car make/model, and why they were on the list. The bad date sheets would be passed out twice a week to give people a "sense of who to look out for".

Rather than using a physical sheet with dangerous individuals' information, Faith recalls there being a website where sex workers could screen their clients. One could type a phone number into the site and would pull up a match if there was one. The "feedback" for each person listed on the site would range from very positive, to very negative, and everything in between. The site has since been taken down as it was rendered illegal by certain anti-prostitution laws. Shutting down these sites which the sex work community uses as a form of harm reduction is yet another way in which the criminal legal system indirectly harms sex workers (Albright & D'Adamo, 2017). By stripping them of a way to verify their clients, the criminal legal system forces sex workers to resort to riskier, more dangerous means of conducting their work ("Is Sex Work Decriminalization the Answer," 2020).

Faith expresses various less conventional methods of self-protection in lieu of law enforcement. She identifies one of these methods as "blending in". Part of her strategy involved passing and going to great lengths to make sure that others outside of the trans community did not know she was a trans woman. This provided protection for her as well as her husband, as she expressed fearing that her husband would face harassment from his peers if they discovered he was with a trans woman. Not only did she place emphasis on passing, but Faith also made it a point to go out of her way to dissociate herself from those in the trans community who were more likely to face harassment. She explains that when she went out to bars, clubs, etc. in her free time, she would avoid being closely associated with trans women who "weren't passable" as that would put her at risk of harassment by association. Instead, she associated more with cisgender women in her community at such times. Seeing this, other members of the trans community assumed she did so because she was "bougie" or felt that she was too good for them. Rather, Faith explained her actions derived from "a sense of survival."

At other times, Faith played into certain stereotypes of trans and Black identities and leveraged them to her advantage. Being a trans woman, many of her clients interpreted her as more dominant and assumed a submissive role in their interactions with her. This perception of her as dominant was emphasized by the fact that she was Black, as Black bodies are often interpreted as hypermasculine and aggressive (Cacho, 2012 and Davis, 1986). That stereotype of Black bodies, which has historically functioned to exclude Black women from the hegemonic ideal of womanhood (Fischer, 2022 and Snorton, 2017), secured Faith's safety as a sex worker as being in a "dominatrix" role, as opposed to a more submissive one, gave her a greater sense of control over interactions with clients.

Aside from taking advantage of various perceptions of her identity, Faith explains having used clever deception to dissuade would-be robbers from targeting her. In her home, which she primarily operated out of, she employed a fake home security system. The system didn't alert the police when it was set off, but simply made a loud noise to startle intruders. When bringing clients to her house, she would shut the door behind them, enter a code on a keypad to arm the system, and tell inquiring dates, "That's just my ADT system making sure that you can't get out without me letting you out." Faith's fake alarm system discouraged most of the people who intended to rob her. As soon as she would arm the system, the men who intended to harm her would confess they had no intention of paying her for her services and ask to be let out. For an added layer of security, Faith used an app on her phone that allowed her to receive fake calls. She scheduled fake calls which she would answer a few minutes after meeting clients. The app allowed users to input a script which would be read aloud with an AI voice by the computer on the other end of the line. Faith used a male voice for her script and pretended to be on the phone with a pimp who she implied was nearby and capable of protecting her if someone tried to rob her, assault her, or shortchange her for her services.

Faith developed these myriad methods of protecting herself by taking careful note of the negative experiences of other Black, trans sex workers and learning from their misfortunes. While explaining the ways she devised her plans, she says,

> there's a smart girl, there's a dumb girl and there's a wise girl.... [A] dumb girl never learns from their mistakes.... [A] smart girl learns from her own mistakes. But a wise girl doesn't let none of that happens to them. A wise girl learns from other people's mistakes. And I was always that girl. I always saw the things that happened in other people and their situations. There's a certain blame the victim mentality here. The point is that this mentality so permeates our society that it is internalized even by those who are victimized and used to differentiate within the group.

This reflects hegemonic views which place emphasis on the actions of the individual rather than the flaws of larger institutions. Faith's statement conveys a victim blaming mentality that places the onus of safety on individual sex workers rather than institutions, such as the criminal legal system, that are ostensibly intended to protect them. This is not to say that Faith intentionally blames other victimized sex workers or does not herself acknowledge systemic shortcomings - she makes it quite clear throughout the interview that the criminal legal system is sorely lacking in its ability and willingness to help sex workers - rather, this demonstrates that the hyperindividualistic mentality characteristic of White, heteronormative culture permeates our society so deeply that it is internalized even by those who are victimized, who then use it to differentiate themselves from others within their community.

In regard to other tactics for promoting their own safety, all respondents express either carrying weapons or being around other Black, trans sex workers that carried weapons for protection. Self-defense implements, such as stun guns and pepper spray (mace), are fairly common and all respondents report having carried at least one of them on their persons when working. Some, like Violet, carried knives to defend against violence. Violet details a dangerous encounter where she was forced to use her knife. A client whose car she'd entered held her at knife point and attempted to force her purse away from her. To distract him, Violet began talking to the man to get him to drop his guard. Once she saw an opportunity, she pulled out her own knife and stabbed him in the chest before fleeing to safety. When caught without a weapon on her person, Violet reports having to fight bare-handed against those who viewed the 5'4" tall woman as an easy target.

Grace herself carried mace and a switch blade on her when working the streets, but also reports working with other sex workers to stash makeshift weapons in her area. She recalls having worked near a "drug house", the outside of which her and others would litter with "metal poles" and anything with enough weight to be used as an improvised weapon. She states,

> but what's a pipe to a gun, you know? What's a pipe that's leaning against the house gonna do when you're inside of a car with a knife to your neck? You know what I mean? But those were the type of measures that we tried to take.

Grace is very aware that, despite her and her peers' extensive attempts at ensuring their safety, it was still inadequate compared to the security she would have enjoyed had she been able to rely on law enforcement for help. Rather than having the criminal legal system at her back to aid her in a crisis or discourage other from victimizing her, she was instead left with a metal pipe that would inexorably be out of reach and of little use if and when she was confronted by someone with a firearm or a knife.

Faith likewise explains that aside from blades, many sex workers would "make their own weapons" which they would carry for protection. Many sex workers carried firearms for self-defense. Olivia states she was "the only one who doesn't carry a gun in [her] friend group," opting instead to carry mace and a blade. Trans sex workers around Grace would also purchase firearms, but notes they had to do so illegally as many vendors in her area would refuse to sell firearms to trans people. Similarly, although Olivia claims it has recently become easier, many in her community encountered difficulties acquiring firearms or licenses to carry due to stereotypes of trans people as mentally unstable and therefore dangerous. Despite known statistics about the rates of mass shootings perpetrated by White, cis men who are often mentally ill ("Public mass shootings," 2022), Black, trans women are identified as a greater threat. This contrast demonstrates that the hegemonic perception of a person's dangerousness is based less on substantial evidence supporting the view and more on the person's presumed ability to conform to White, cis-heteropatriarchal norms.

Overall, sex workers, regardless of gender identity, sexuality, or race, typically carry some sort of weapon for self-defense. Grace notes that while Black and trans individuals are more likely to encounter violence, the sex industry (particularly street work) is dangerous for anyone involved. Meanwhile, Olivia clarifies that while almost all of the sex workers around her carry tools for self-defense, Black sex workers typically have to carry more lethal implements than White ones to keep themselves safe. According to her, while White sex workers most often carry stun guns or pepper spray, Black sex workers are more likely to carry knives and firearms. Some even carry guns in the open, either in their hands or their bras, to appear more intimidating and immediately ward off dangerous parties. This intentional display of aggression emphasizes hegemonic perceptions of Black sex workers who are already perceived to be more violent than others because of racist stereotypes characterizing them as such (Alexander, 2020 and Cacho, 2012). It is due to these stereotypes, however, that, despite helping to secure their safety, carrying weapons sometimes places sex workers at higher risk of encountering law enforcement and abuse from officers. Violet explains that carrying weapons often leads to police perceiving sex workers as more violent than they already do, compelling the officers to act more aggressively toward what they see as a threat. In other words, not only do police, through their unreliability, force sex workers to employ violent forms of self-defense, but they punish them for taking measures to protect themselves. This demonstrates a cycle of oppression where individuals turn to desperate measures to survive and are criminalized for it, therefore making them even more reliant on dangerous methods of survival. In this way, the criminal legal system functions as a biopolitical mechanism for disallowing the lives of sex workers, especially Black, trans sex workers, thus impeding their ability to live healthier and safer. This demonstrates that the system functions to enforce social control according to hegemonic hierarchies, not to encourage justice or ensure the safety of its people.

CHAPTER V

NOTHING ABOUT US WITHOUT US – WHAT NEEDS TO BE DONE

The final theme that arose during conversation with study's respondents are needs they express on behalf of the Black, trans and sex working community as well as actions they think should be taken to ensure greater safety for the community. These needs are primarily centered around cultural changes regarding perceptions of sex workers and Black, trans individuals that would result in a greater understanding of their lived experiences and struggles. Participants also express necessary changes to the criminal legal system in order to make sex workers safer. Overall, the needs of the Black, trans and sex working community expressed by respondents consist of: 1) the need for sex workers to be seen and respected as autonomous beings; 2) myriad changes to the criminal legal system; 3) persistent, outspoken advocacy and activism; 4) intersectional approaches to activism; and 5) proper minority representation in organizations/movements focused on aiding sex workers. These needs run counter to the goal of the criminal legal system, which is to impose regulatory controls on sex workers, particularly Black, trans sex workers, who deviate from White, cis-heteropatriarchal norms. To that end, safety for Black, trans sex workers necessitates the deconstruction of not only hegemonic norms that rely on a social hierarchy, at the bottom of which non-heteronormative genders and sexualities reside, but also of the criminal legal system such that it is replaced by institutions that reformulate society in a non-hierarchical manner.

Sex Worker Autonomy

When not being demonized as corrupt sexual deviants and predators, sex workers are, more often than not, infantilized. Hegemonic perceptions of sex workers include stereotypes of them as victims, damsels in distress (usually White women) who are coerced into doing sex work by someone seeking to take advantage of them (usually men). Without a doubt, sex trafficking is a very real and prevalent social problem, and many find themselves coerced or forced into the sex industry. However, conversations with this study's respondents show that the story of the sex trafficking victim is not the exclusive experience of those in the sex industry, nor is it even the primary experience of those who specifically work as escorts, prostitutes, "street girls", etc. Each of the respondent's choices to pursue sex work was an intentional and calculated decision made by someone who was simply doing what it took to ensure their own survival. Rather than speaking to the proclivities of individuals, this denotes systemic failures as the reason some choose to participate in sex work. In the case of Black, trans sex workers, they are subjugated by hegemonic norms which result not only in their expulsion from legal employment, but their victimization, both directly and indirectly, by the criminal legal system. The actions of broader institutions are what influence them to participate in sex work and subsequently encounter victimization.

Not only does sex work present a method of survival for individuals, it supports the survival of entire communities. As detailed earlier, Shanae Adams, a therapist and educator who specializes in sex-positivity, explained during a seminar that sex work financially supported the ballroom scene on the East coast, especially following the Harlem Renaissance. Sex work provided food, shelter, and basic needs for members of the community. Kim confirms that "sex work is holding down many communities," and Grace and Violet agree, claiming that sex work has proved especially valuable to the Black, trans community which has historically been excluded from rights, privileges, and social safety nets which other demographic groups have been, to varying degrees, allowed to enjoy.

Having been confronted with extensive employment discrimination, deprived of adequate support systems, or demonized for their "always already" sexualized gender and racial identities, the women in this study made the rational choice to rely on sex work for survival. Despite potentially having to face criminalization, abuse, and violence, they still needed to eat and to have shelter. Furthermore, as demonstrated by Faith and Grace's experiences, Black, trans folk are also at risk of criminalization, abuse, and violence in legal employment anyways. Sex work provides them with a profession that is not only more lucrative at times, but also provides them a degree of independence which they are not afforded by most other forms of employment. Grace elaborates:

> And the reality is as an escort or as a sex worker on the streets or as a porn star or anything that you do in the sex work industry, honestly, the sex worker has the upper hand because we get to choose who we want to sleep with. I don't have to jump in every car. I don't have to take every… you know what I mean? So, I get to choose, pick and choose in that sense. Also, I get to tell you what my worth is, you know, like you can offer me whatever the fuck you want, but I don't have to take that. So, there is a form of power that comes behind it.

As she points out, Black, trans women are given independence and agency in the sex trade that they are not afforded in other areas of work. Sex workers determine for themselves what kind of work they do, when they work, and with whom they work. Furthermore, they dictate their own "worth," an act which contradicts hegemonic norms that determine people's worths according to their ability to conform to White heteronormativity.

Grace also notes the absurdity of the fact that an activity often legally done between two consenting adults is criminalized once it involves an exchange of money. She points out that people "hook up with random people that they may never see again and don't get a penny out of it. But because someone charges for that, there's something wrong with that." The key difference between sex workers and those in other forms of employment, she explains, is the fact that the former involves a subject that people are frequently shamed for: sex. As we've seen, this is especially the case for marginalized communities such as Black or trans folk whose very identities are fetishized and seen as sexually deviant by nature (Davis, 1986; hooks, 2014; and Snorton, 2017).

Sexuality is typically considered a point of shame in hegemonic society (Mogul et al., 2011), but Fischer (2022) points out that the shamefulness lies not in sexuality, but in specifically non-normative displays of sexuality. They explain that White womanhood, and by extension White women's sexuality, is valorized in society because White women are viewed as sites of reproduction for White heteronormativity. Non-normative sexualities, such as that of Black people, trans people, and sex workers, however, are denigrated. In turn, those who participate in sex work, especially Black, trans individuals, are seen as contributing nothing to society. While other traits characteristic of humanity, such as strength, athleticism, intelligence, creativity, ingenuity, or dexterity, are seen as contributive to society, sexuality is regarded as a trait which either adds nothing to society or actively detracts from it when it is presented in a non-normative body. In this context, biopolitics are deployed in relation to particular (i.e., non-White, non-heteronormative) populations in such a way that their public displays of gender and sexuality are institutionally reprimanded in order to maintain their position at the bottom of the hegemonic hierarchy. My respondents and other advocates for sex worker rights assert that sex work, like any other form of labor, is *work* and should be respected as such (Global Network of Sex Work Projects, 2017). Doing so not only deconstructs social hierarchies that delineate Black and trans sexualities as deviant, but also encourages the respect of sex workers as autonomous beings who make conscious, rational decisions to enter their professions to secure their basic needs.

There are those who would take issue with the imperatives of deconstructing shame surrounding non-heteronormative sexualities and respecting sex worker autonomy, claiming that it would exacerbate the issue of sex trafficking; however, there is little evidence to support that claim. As this study and other works demonstrate, sex workers who intentionally choose to participate in the sex trade are distinct from those who are forced or coerced into sex work (Fitzgerald et al., 2015). Efforts to acknowledge the validity of sex work as a form of labor destigmatize the work and in turn make it safer for those who willingly choose to participate ("Is Sex Work Decriminalization the Answer," 2020). Furthermore, there is research which suggests that such efforts, such as those supporting decriminalization, also improve conditions for those who are forced or coerced into sex work (Albright & D'Adamo, 2017).

Education, Abolition, and Other Solutions

According to Violet, the largest problem Black, trans sex workers face in their daily lives is discrimination against their identities, considering that anti-Black, anti-trans, and anti-sex worker beliefs and cultural norms are the root of various forms of violence, harassment, and discrimination the community encounters. Respondents faced extensive transphobic employment discrimination, which prevented them from finding legal employment; even when they were able to attain legal employment, transphobic harassment and abuse from coworkers and bosses made working conditions intolerable. Often, as their stories reveal, these hostile environments are intentionally created by transphobic others who seek to remove them from the workplace. Violence respondents encountered was framed and exacerbated by their racial identities as police saw them as more threatening and potential robbers saw them as more vulnerable, more lucrative targets. Their occupations as sex workers conveyed to others that they could be targeted for violence with impunity because police were more likely to accuse the victims of wrongdoing than to help them. As people displaying non-normative sexualities, Black, trans sex workers are not viewed as valid victims because their sexuality is not valued by hegemonic society in the way that heteronormative sexualities are valued.

Considering that their largest problem is discrimination stemming primarily from ignorance and bigotry, it comes as no surprise that education is identified by respondents as the most significant way to change the criminal legal system as well as the current cultural zeitgeist. Among the forms of education necessary, Grace specifies the people must be more educated about Black, trans experiences in the sex trade, as well as the history and acknowledgment of sex work as a valid form of work. Knowledge of these histories is essential to validating, in the eyes of dominant society, the status of sex workers as autonomous and capable of contributing to society as much as any other individual.

Such ideas, Grace explains, should be taught both within and outside of the criminal legal system. Agents of the criminal legal system must be educated to know how to properly interact with sex workers. She also asserts that the general public must be educated so as to change what acts are deemed as acceptable to be criminalized. For example, such education can prohibit behaviors such as talking to strangers, walking outside, and waving to others on the street, all of which can constitute criminal acts according to manifestation and assignation statutes (Brydum, 2014; Mogul et al., 2011; and "Prostitution," 2022) from being seen a criminalizable acts. While this approach may alleviate issues of discrimination on the level of individual officers who receive the education, it does not necessarily address the larger structural problem's inherent to the criminal legal system, such as the fact that it was designed to reinforce racial and gender hierarchies. The logic behind this individualistic educational approach to social change is that societal institutions largely conform to the dominant beliefs of the society in which they are situated, meaning that in order to change an institution's ideological approach, one must first change the ideology of the dominant social groups surrounding it. Following this logic, in order for the criminal legal system to adequately accept sex work as a valid profession and sex workers as contributing members of society, these views must first be adopted by the general population.

This educational approach seeks to alter the ways in which the state regulates sex to achieve biopolitical goals. By using discursive strategies to change dominant views of sex work, the approach aims to remove sex work as a target for state regulation (Claggett, 2023). While this may shift the dominant perception of sex workers as not contributive to society, it would still leave the criminal legal system intact. With the criminal legal system still operational as an institutional mechanism for social control, it would be susceptible to discursive strategies which seek to denigrate sex work and reinforce White, cis-heteronormative ideals. For this reason, while education is important to destigmatize sex work and lessen the victimization of Black, trans sex workers, it does not necessarily curb the criminal legal system's ability to exercise disciplinary power for the sake of reinforcing hegemonic norms.

Violet concurs with Grace's emphasis on education, adding that those who already wish to aid marginalized communities must "know what they face in order for them to be able to help those communities." Additionally, she states that the general population must be made aware of the anti-Black, anti-trans beliefs inherent in the criminal legal system, in order to specifically identify and correct the various forms of discrimination executed by agents of the system. Violet's perspective comes closer to addressing the issue discussed previously regarding the criminal legal system's biopolitical power as a mechanism for social control. Elaborating to others how the criminal legal system is inherently designed to enforce racist, transphobic norms could bring its legitimacy into question and staunch its influence as a social institution.

Kim adds that sexual education with emphasis on sex-positivity is crucial to the movement advocating for Black, trans sex worker rights. Having immigrated to the United States from a different country, she comments that there was a marked difference between the discourse surrounding sexuality in both countries. Discussions regarding sex education, sexuality, and sex-positivity are limited in the U.S. compared to the discussions prevalent in the Oceanic country from which she emigrated. She sees this as a limiting factor in the progression of sex worker rights in the United States. The silence surrounding discussions of sexuality, particularly the designation of non-heteronormative sexualities as taboo topics, allows dominant narratives regarding sexuality to dominant the public mind. In other words, as a biopolitical mechanism for social control, the silencing of disparate, non-normative perspectives removes any obstacles keeping hegemonic norms from being prioritized.

Respondents also discuss some reforms to the criminal legal system that could improve the living conditions of sex workers and Black, trans folk in general. Some mention LGBTQ liaison, officers who are part of the queer community and are therefore better equipped to handle issues involving other members of that community. The police department in Violet's city employed LGBTQ liaisons, which she says led to a noticeable improvement in police treatment of trans individuals and sex workers. For example, when a sex worker was a victim of a crime, LGBTQ liaisons would see to it that the case was taken seriously rather than offhandedly dismissed. Violet states,

> they [LGBTQ liaisons] would step in and they would actually do the job instead of which the regular police would just basically brush it under the rug or try to blame the sex worker. This unit actually did their job.

While her city did not have specifically assigned LGBTQ liaisons, Faith points out that there were queer folk within her local police force that were "trying to make a change from within." However, she clarified, the queer officers attempting to change police treatment of queer folk are often suppressed and are themselves at risk of harassment and abuse within their own profession. Despite placing themselves in positions where they are capable of effecting change, queer officers are still a minority and are easily silenced by a homophobic and transphobic majority. This suggests that it is not enough to simply have queer officers present in the force. As is the case with Violet's city, the police department itself must take steps to improve police interactions with queer individuals and specifically appoint its queer officers to positions of authority where they are better able to bring about that change. Even when institutional policies that elevate the voices of queer officers are put in place, however, the criminal legal system remains an institution operating under carceral logics inherently meant to oppress non-normative bodies (Lamble, 2015). Despite the presence of queer officers, there is nothing to preclude the system from adopting homonormative perspectives that, while welcoming of some queer and trans bodies, still operate within a hierarchy that prioritizes adherence to racialized, gendered norms (Stryker, 2008).

Grace mentions a legal reform that improved police interactions with sex workers. This reform did not take place in the city where she actively participated in sex work. Instead, it came about in the city in which she currently lives and conducts activism for sex worker rights. A few years ago, her state's criminal legal system ratified a law enforcement policy stating that if a sex worker were to report a crime committed against them, they were to be treated as a regular victim and could not be charged for prostitution during the time of reporting. When advocating for this policy to be put in place, Grace often cited her experiences as a sex worker where she was violently victimized, yet still unable to rely on police for fear of judgment or punishment. She notes that while anti-sex worker discrimination is still present within her current state's law enforcement, the policy has brought about a notable improvement in the ability of sex workers to rely on police. This conclusion is in line with extensive research which shows that one of the primary reasons sex workers choose not to call police for help in times of crisis is that they fear they will be criminalized despite being a victim (Nadal et al., 2014; Serpe & Nadal, 2017; and Sherman et al., 2015).

Faith notes that police officers need to be held accountable for their actions. Grace expresses a similar sentiment, stating that if the aim is to reform the justice system, "then there needs to be more penalization for people who step outside of what their job titles are." In other words, officers who break laws with impunity, inflicting violence on others - like those officers who abused this study's participants - must be penalized. Even when such acts are reported, the survivors' stories are usually immediately doubted, and their assaults swept under the rug. The ability to rely on the criminal legal system for protection is essential for guaranteeing the safety of sex workers, Black, trans folk, and other marginalized communities (Nadal et al., 2014). The police cannot be relied upon if violent offenders within the system itself are not properly held accountable and stripped of their positions of power which empower them to commit such violence (Stinson et al., 2020). However, it is important not that this approach of penalizing violent officers involves further investment in the carceral criminal legal system when marginalized communities would be better served through movement away from such a system and toward community-based alternatives (Davis et al., 2022)

The most important reform to Faith, which is also mentioned by Grace and Violet, is the complete decriminalization of sex work. Decriminalization is the most vital step toward ensuring the safety of sex workers. Faith explains that when sex work is criminalized,

> it pushes the community to have to do these sexual acts and behind these closed doors and unsafe places that puts us at risk of getting robbed, killed and, you know, and the worst.

As Faith points out, sex work criminalization forces sex workers to take riskier measures. Research demonstrates that much of the legislation that targets sex work does not actually make sex workers safer and instead places them in positions of greater danger (Albright & D'Adamo,

2017). Legislative efforts in the U.S., such as SESTA/FOSTA, take away sex workers' ability to safely conduct sex work by vetting their clients and making informed decisions ("Is Sex Work Decriminalization the Answer," 2020).

Some areas of the United States have partially decriminalized sex work. Grace's city, for example, does not criminalize victims of sex trafficking or sex workers with pimps, but still criminalizes independent sex workers. The problem with this approach is that it is not immediately clear to police officers who is and is not a victim of sex trafficking. A person who has been sex trafficked may therefore still become involved in the criminal legal system, and even if the charges are eventually dropped, the initial arrest will still appear on their record. Furthermore, this law does nothing to make the living conditions of non-trafficked sex workers safer; they are still persecuted by the criminal legal system as usual.

Some countries, such as Germany and Singapore, have legalized prostitution only in certain circumstances. In those countries, one can legally sell sex only if they have proper certification, are registered with the government, or are working out of state-owned brothels. As activists have found, however, this presents barriers to those who live in poverty and rely on sex work for survival as they may lack the resources necessary to become registered. Just as we have seen with this study, such regulations criminalized the most vulnerable populations above all others. As discussed previously, the disproportionate targeting of vulnerable populations is a biopolitical strategy that benefits hegemonic hierarchies by maintaining the existence of a permanent lower class consisting of non-heteronormative bodies (Ferguson, 2003 and Foucault, 1990). Other countries, such as Canada and France, have legalized prostitution, but still criminalize the purchase of sex. While this is ostensibly beneficial, as sex workers are no longer criminalized in those areas, these laws work to deprive sex workers of their income. If clients are criminalized, this makes it more difficult for those who see selling sex as their only option to find work. Therefore, such laws make it difficult for those relying on sex work to survive. Without proper social systems in place to financially support marginalized communities (thus removing the need to rely on sex work in the first place) these laws do more harm than good to the sex working community.

Partial decriminalization has been shown time and time again to be inadequate. As such, activists for sex worker rights call for the *complete* decriminalization of sex work (Global Network of Sex Work Projects, 2017 and Robarge et al., 2016). The concept of decriminalization revolves around a harm reduction approach to public health. Movements for decriminalization prioritize the health and safety of those in the sex trade over all else. Once again, decriminalization of the act of selling sex does not make sex trafficking more permissible, similar to how other forms of labor being legal does not make slavery in those trades permissible.

Decriminalization is not enough, however, and steps must be taken to address the systemic failures that create the need to rely on sex work for survival in the first place. One such way of addressing these concerns is the abolition of the current criminal legal system. During the interviews, I asked each participant to elaborate their thoughts on abolition of the current criminal legal system as a solution to the oppression of Black, trans sex workers and those stigmatized as such. When asked about her thoughts regarding reform versus abolition of the system, Grace expresses a frustration and cynicism felt deeply by many in the sex industry. She believed that there would always be individuals with hateful ideologies that, if given the power of a law enforcement officer, would allow those biases to seep into their work where it would negatively impact the communities they're meant to serve. Recalling a video she'd seen recently where a Black, trans woman was ripped out of her car and violently beaten by an officer, she comments how police seem to always turn a blind eye to such incidents. It's that same willful ignorance, she claims, that allows unarmed Black people to be killed in the street, cases of trans murder victims to be swept under the rug, and violent perpetrators to get slaps on the wrist for using a panic defense after harming a trans person. Grace puts it succinctly and poignantly when she says,

> There is no silver lining for justice. If we continue to just try to reform, there's got to be something different.

Grace's perspective partially reflects dominant ideologies about police misconduct and brutality which place emphasis on "bad apples" within the system as the primary perpetrators of police violence (Alexander, 2020). While she is correct that abolition of the current system is necessary, it is not because of the presence of racist, transphobic individuals. Surely, if this were the case, then the amount of "good cops" in the system, such as the LGBTQ liaisons, would counter the influence of the "bad cops." However, the problem is systemic in nature because the criminal legal system was intentionally designed to be an oppressive, regulatory institution that targets non-normative populations (Cacho, 2012 and Lamble, 2015).

Faith is a little more hesitant when it came to the thought of abolition, claiming she was unsure whether she was "ready to live in a world where there's no police involved." The threats of violence she faces do not come solely from the criminal legal system. She, and many other Black, trans folk in the sex industry, are at particularly high risk of being targeted by other civilians for robbery, harassment, abuse, and assault. Looking back on her experiences, she acknowledges that although the vast majority of her experiences with the police were negative, there were still some situations where they actually helped her. When it came down to it, Faith simply does not feel confident that other members of her community were in a position to be able to help each other in lieu of the police. Abolition doesn't feel realistic to her, as she believes society and its members have a lot of "growing" to do in terms of their knowledge of and spiritual connection to others. What Faith may not understand about abolitionism, however, is that the movement does not simply intend to dismantle the prison industrial complex (PIC) in one great instance but sees abolition as a gradual process in which the PIC will be replaced with other, carefully structured institutions. In the book *Abolition. Feminism. Now.* (2022), Davis and colleagues hold that abolition is "as much about the work that focuses on building and experimenting as it [is] on what must be dismantled" (p. 51). That is to say the goal of abolition, as a philosophy and a movement, is not simply to deconstruct the current criminal legal system, but to create "preventative, community-based responses" to crime victimization and other sources of harm to public health. These responses, in contrast to the pervading system, would be capable of addressing the myriad forms of harm endemic to communities which have their roots in racist, gendered, colonial discrimination. In other words, the crux of the abolitionist movement is to shift from a reliance on a carceral criminal legal system to a series of social systems designed to address systemic failures in society, such as the inability of the criminal legal system to promote the public health of marginalized communities with its punitive methods.

Grace and Violet both agree that the Black, trans community and the sex work community would be better served if we relied more on other systems for certain needs than we did the police. Grace explains that,

> it's not like officers are trained to be counselors. It's not like they're even trained on sensitivity issues.... Like they literally are thrown out on the street with all of the aggressions and all of the everything that they've built up over their years. They're given a gun and a badge and thrown out in the streets. And there's no vetting that goes on to see what people's political or ideology ideas are or how they feel about racism....

As she points out, training for police officers is extremely limited given the breadth of the issues for which they are relied upon. On average, police across the country receive less than six months of basic training (twenty-one weeks). To gain the authority to issue fines, arrest people, and kill with near impunity, one need only train for an average of 840 hours, around half the time it takes for one to become a licensed barber or cosmetologist (Reaves, 2016). Despite the relative dearth of training they undergo, police officers are relied upon a litany of issues which they are often not equipped to handle, such as mental health crises, sexual assaults, medical emergencies, and even animal control, to name a few. Furthermore, police are not vetted for dangerous ideologies or violent tendencies that should give pause to anyone thinking of granting them state authority. For example, there is a concerning prevalence of White supremacists in the U.S. police force (FBI, 2006 and German, 2020), and police officers have been shown to be more likely than the general population to be perpetrators of domestic violence (Cheema, 2016 and Goodmark, 2015). These observations mean that it is not only ineffective to rely so heavily on police for a wide range of social issues, but it can also prove detrimental to society.

The three primary tools police utilize are fines, arrests, and force/violence (up to, and including, murder), none of which are at all useful to marginalized communities who need financial stability, medical care, and cultural understanding above all else (Alexander, 2020 and Davis et al., 2022). Ticketing someone is not going to magically alleviate them of the need to rely on sex work for survival. Arresting people isn't going to repair the rippling effects of centuries of systemic racism. Harming or killing with state-sanctioned violence isn't going to give trans folk livable wages in places of employment where they aren't at risk of abuse. The police are not equipped to adequately assuage society's ailments. The tools at their disposal, when used incorrectly and irresponsibly (as they are now), can only exacerbate the issues and push marginalized communities deeper into crisis. When viewing law enforcement's punitive methods through a biopolitical lens, it is revealed that their tools are not meant to provide aid or promote public health at all. Instead, they are extremely effective at impeding the health of entire communities, suppressing displays of non-normative sexuality, and reinforcing hegemonic norms of dominance (Davis et al., 2022; Ferguson, 2003; and Fischer, 2022). Diverting resources from the police into other social systems that are equipped to handle a wide range of problems (i.e., education, childcare, medical care, affordable living, etc.) is the aim of the abolitionist movement. Faith's concerns are warranted, considering the current state of the world, but abolitionist groups emphasize that the shift to a society that doesn't rely on the present punitive legal system must be gradual and carefully thought out rather than instantaneous and unstable (Davis et al., 2022). It is this eventuality which abolitionists build toward that others, like Violet and Grace, see as the best future for Black, trans folk in the sex trade.

Persistent Activism and Intersectionality

The most consistently discussed needs for the Black, trans sex work community were persistent, outspoken advocacy and activism. Kim reveals that the progress made thus far for trans sex worker rights is not coincidental. The progress did not arise from a teleological progression of social ideals that culminated in greater acceptance of marginalized communities (Davis et al., 2022). Rather, the changes in ideology and protections for trans sex workers have been strategically fought for, tooth and nail, by activists within the sex trade and their advocates without. In order to gain further rights for sex workers, particularly Black, trans ones, activism must be continual, relentless, and loud.

With her experience as an activist for Black, trans folks Grace notes that non-Black allies would not have taken up the cause had Grace and others in her community not spoken up about their oppression. Those in positions of social privilege are often blind to the struggles of those lacking such privilege because dominant society's most powerful tool for oppression is the invisibilization of marginalized peoples, their experiences, and their epistemologies. As such, Grace emphasizes that "as Black, trans women, we have to continue to use our voice to call out the bullshit." By speaking up and bringing awareness, the Black, trans community makes their struggles impossible to ignore.

Kim explains that for some working in sex worker rights activism, there is a concern that there is little public support for the issue. However, citing a campaign she ran with her Black, trans colleague, Tia, who had been wrongfully arrested for prostitution, she recalls having been surprised by the amount of support they received. In just a day, they had fund-raised over two thousand dollars and discovered that there was international support for their activism that they would not have found had they not drawn attention to the issue. These statements demonstrate that there is potential for widespread, emphatic support for sex worker rights, but that such support only arises with concerted efforts to spread awareness about the issues surrounding those rights. Faith similarly mentions advocacy from individuals outside affected communities but insists that their advocacy needs to go "a step further." According to her, "we don't need allyships. We need co-conspirators." In other words, those wishing to give support to the Black, trans and sex working communities achieve little by standing and watching from the sidelines. She asserts,

> we need people that are actually with us. That is willing to take the blame with us. That's willing to stand there for us. And that's willing to, you know, stand in the forefront while we're in the back.

Of particular importance to her is the idea of those with privilege utilizing that privilege to make gains for marginalized groups. When advocating for social justice, an action that carries varying degrees of risk, it makes little sense to place the most vulnerable at the forefront where they are in the greatest danger. Hence, the need for co-conspirators to "stand in the forefront while we're in the back."

Violet asserts that the fight for sex worker and Black, trans rights must be persistent and relentless. For her, with the Black, trans sex working community being constantly at risk and in danger, the only option for survival is to continue to fight. The alternative is to give up and allow the system to kill them. One of Kim's colleagues, Tia, phrased it poignantly when she said, "[If] I back down, it doesn't make any difference because they'll be coming to get me tomorrow anyway.... I could lose my life now, but I could lose my life tomorrow." For Faith, however, advocating for sex worker rights can be a struggle in itself, especially for those in the sex industry or who are a part of other marginalized communities. She points out the weighty stigma that comes along within even being considered in proximity to sex work, stating,

> I think it's an embarrassing stigma for me, even for me as an advocate now, today. Every time I'm advocating for sex workers rights and having a conversation, I still freeze up a little because I'm always like praying and hoping that I don't get embarrassed in a way that demonizes who I am, or would like literally back me into a corner and never want to do this again. Because I feel that there's - you know, there's evil people, obviously, that has ways of twisting and turning what you say, or what you're trying to say, or just using their knowledge and their education to try and like publicly shame you and make you look stupid.

Individuals who lack Faith's lived experience devalue her knowledge, dismissing her as someone who, as a sex worker, has comparatively little to contribute to society. Because it is so stigmatized, outsiders tend to disregard the autonomy of sex workers and the valuable first-hand knowledge they possess. This dismissal, in turn, can lead sex workers, activists, and advocates to internalize feeling of shame, embarrassment, or inferiority about their work. This issue can be somewhat alleviated by the strategy Faith mentioned prior, whereby those with privilege position themselves to take the brunt of the risk involved rather than offloading it onto the most vulnerable among them.

Finally, respondents express the need for intersectional approaches to activism that included adequate representation of marginalized communities in positions of leadership. Kim expresses that, when she moved to the United States to continue the sex worker rights activism she'd conducted in her previous country, she was astonished to see how few Black, trans folk held positions of leadership in activist organizations, especially considering their large presence in the sex working community. As an organizer, she has always emphasized that the fight for sex worker rights should always come "hand in hand with trans rights." Trans individuals are regularly fetishized, hypersexualized, and assumed to be sex workers, regardless of whether or not they're involved in the sex industry, just for being transgender in public. Despite this, organizations even in Kim's home country tended to distance themselves from the subject of trans people and instead focused on cisgender women. At that time, she reports, there was "tremendous pushback on the trans community" due to transphobic perceptions from cis women who "[didn't] want to mix with men."

Despite the ostensible lack of relation between sex worker rights and trans rights, however, Violet emphasizes that sex worker oppression, trans oppression, and even Black oppression are all connected. It is imperative for Black, trans and sex worker rights to be fought for in tandem for three reasons. First, the oppression of all three communities has its origins in White, cis-heteropatriarchal domination and thus share common causes for their existence. As such, if only one group has acquired rights, the root problem has not been addressed, meaning all of the communities are still at risk of oppression (Davis et al., 2022). Second, the categories of Black, trans and sex worker are not mutually exclusive, and many occupy multiple. This means, for example, if only Black rights are attained, Black individuals who are trans and/or sex workers would still experience oppression (Mogul et al., 2011). And third, with its reliance on neoliberal politics to stay dominant, White, cis-heteropatriarchal society has created an environment in which acquiring rights is seen as a zero-sum game which requires groups to assume the position of oppressor and subjugate outgroups (Cacho, 2012; Hollibaugh & Weiss, 2015; and Stryker, 2008). This ideology is unsustainable for any dominant social group as it creates the very same groups which will eventually fight to end its dominance. In other words, only promoting the rights for one community (i.e., Black, trans, or sex workers) inevitably necessitates the oppression of the others. The solution, therefore, must be to do away with the notion that, when advocating for the rights of a given people, only one group should be supported at a time (Ferguson, 2019). Activism for any group is most effective when it addresses the root causes of oppression and advocates for the rights of all who find themselves oppressed by a given hegemony.

Part of an intersectional approach means placing persons with a diverse array of backgrounds in positions of power and influence where their voices and unique experience can be used and shared to the best of their ability. As stated previously by Kim, however, the placement of Black, trans individuals in leadership positions in the sex worker rights movement is tenuous. When she arrived in the United States and contacted organizations here, she claimed that nearly every person in leadership was White, none of them were trans, and none of them were sex workers. When she took it upon herself to invite Black, trans folk in the sex working community to positions of leadership, some responded with surprise, stating that no one had ever asked them to do so before. On the other hand, Faith and Violet felt that sex worker rights organizations in their areas did have adequate representation of other marginalized communities in their leadership. Violet knows of multiple trans women in organizations that lead the work in fighting for trans youth's rights, women's rights, and others. In fact, she herself is the co-director of an organization that aids a coalition of sex worker rights groups. Faith, while not in a place of leadership herself, knows of multiple organizations led by Black, trans folk whose specific aim is to represent and uplift the Black and trans communities.

Unfortunately, Grace's experience is not the same and she feels that the Black, trans representation in organizations near her is lacking. While not occupying a position of leadership in a particular organization, she is still very active in her community as an activist and has placed herself at the forefront of the movement for sex worker rights there. She notes that placing oneself in such a position is especially difficult for people in marginalized communities. As a Black, trans woman involved with the sex trade, she is constantly at risk both from the criminal legal system and others who seek to do her harm. Stepping into power and adopting a role as an activist places individuals at even greater risk because they are now in the spotlight. According to her, for someone in the Black, trans sex working community to want to do that, they "have to get to a place of being fed up." She states,

> You have to get to that point of saying: you know what, I am sick of seeing this. So, if I have to die being one of the people that fight for the rights of people like me, and then that's what I'm gonna do, and I think that's the stage that I got to.

In other words, for someone in an already extremely vulnerable position to be willing to step up as a leader and activist, they must be ready to give their lives for the movement. People in Grace's community, and in the Black, trans community at large, assume such risks when they have been pushed to the absolute limit and placing themselves at risk is the only option available to them. This sentiment reflects a central idea introduced at the beginning of this and emphasized throughout: to survive at whatever cost. Just as Black, trans folk in the sex trade will continue to do sex work as a means to survive, even if it means constantly being in great danger, so too will they risk their lives to advocate for better ones in spite of a system that wants them dead. The fact that they need to be pushed to a certain point before they will be willing to join activist efforts, however, presents a problem in terms of recruiting Black, trans sex workers to positions of leadership. Many will not be willing or able to take the risk. Faith's earlier perspective addresses this to some degree; placing those with privilege in positions where they can act as buffers between vulnerable communities and hegemonic institutions can allow Black, trans folk to take on less risk in taking leadership positions.

This study's participants highlight various changes, reforms, policies, and movements necessary to ensure greater safety and public health for Black, trans sex workers and those criminalized as such. Some involve cultural efforts to change common perceptions of Black, trans folk and sex workers, while others consist of reforms to the criminal legal system and legislation on sex work. Furthermore, interviews with participants include discussions on the utility of abolition versus reform. Finally, respondents emphasize the importance of intersectional approaches to sex worker rights activism that include placing Black, trans sex workers in positions of leadership in the movement. Many of the participants' suggestions focus on confronting the actions and beliefs individuals within the criminal legal system rather than more directly addressing the systemic issues, such as racism, transphobia, and ineffective, punitive methods, that grant law enforcement the power to be so detrimental to marginalized communities. This study addresses these individualistic sentiments by explaining how they reflect dominant perspectives surrounding sex work and Black, trans bodies, and suggests alternatives, such as PIC abolishment, that focus on the deconstruction of White, cis-heteropatriarchal norms that necessitate the maintenance of dehumanizing, hegemonic hierarchies.

Throughout this study I have elaborated the ways in which Black, trans sex workers are more likely to come into contact with the criminal legal system than their White and cisgender counterparts, the direct and indirect forms of violence they face from the system, as well as measures that must be taken to end the violence and promote safety for Black, trans sex workers.

In doing so, I have identified the criminal legal system as an institution designed to promote hegemonic society's biopolitical goals. The system achieves this by exercising disciplinary power in the form of violence against Black, trans sex workers and those stigmatized as such in order to disallow their life, trap them at the bottom of the hegemonic social hierarchy, and reinforce White, cis-heteropatriarchal dominance. The study also contributes to existing research on sex work criminalization by offering in-depth accounts of the lived experiences of Black, trans folk who have been criminalized for sex work and explaining how the intersection of their racial and gender identities informed their experiences with the criminal legal system. Furthermore, my analyses are important to criminal justice scholarship and movements that explore ways to rectify the widespread, negative effects of deeply ingrained, systemic racism and transphobia in the criminal legal system because of how I place criminal justice scholarship in direct conversation with transgender, Black feminist, and queer of color critical theory. This allows me to reveal the inherently racist and transphobic nature of the criminal legal system as I trace its roots to White, heteronormative colonial practices. Moreover, considering the dearth of research on sex work criminalization that focuses specifically on Black, trans people, the breadth of experiences detailed in this study provides a foundation upon which future research can be conducted because it allows for a more comprehensive understanding of experiences that are unique to Black, trans folk as they encounter the criminal legal system.

I encountered several limitations to this study over the course of my research. For example, this study's small sample size limits the range of experiences it is able to encapsulate. With only four participants, it is unlikely that I was able to capture the full range of experiences Black, trans sex workers have when encountering the criminal legal system. Furthermore, experiences of Black, trans sex workers likely differ based on the region of the U.S. they are from. Two of the participants report being from the East coast, one from the South, and one from the West region of the country. Because of this limited coverage, I was unable to glean insight about experiences of Black, trans sex workers from the West coast, the Midwest, or the Northern parts of the country, which may differ somewhat in terms of cultures surrounding sex work as well as legislation. Future research into the criminalization of Black, trans people for sex work should include data from more areas of the U.S. to discern any notable differences in experiences. As stated in the beginning, this study's sample only included trans women. I was thus unable to adequately document the experiences of Black sex workers with other trans identities, such as trans men and nonbinary people. The inclusion of other groups under the trans umbrella is essential to capturing the myriad forms racialized gender oppression manifests for Black, trans sex workers. However, there is very little scholarship focusing specifically on the sex work criminalization of trans men, nonbinary people, or other trans groups, which may be partially due to the fact that trans women are more likely to be criminalized for sex work than other trans persons. Therefore, future research into this study's subject matter should expand upon this limited coverage and document experiences of Black sex workers across the transgender spectrum in order to determine how transphobia in the criminal legal system produces different experiences based on a person's specific identity.

As stated previously, due to the nature of oral history research, this study's findings cannot be considered generalizable. Rather, the utility of my findings resides in the intimate observations of the participants' first-hand experiences. The data collected here, while not generalizable, contains a depth and level of detail which most quantitative methods are unable to attain. It is my intent that other researchers into this study's subject use these data, along with other qualitative sources, as a foundation to guide future research into the criminalization of

Black, trans individuals for sex work. By utilizing my work as a guide, for example, future researchers can modify survey questions to be more specific to Black, trans experiences and capture more relevant data.

In addition to the goals for future research laid out above, later endeavors should examine intersections of transness and other racial identities as they pertain to sex work criminalization. The systemic racism detailed in this study, while bearing many similarities to racism against other racial and ethnic groups, is largely unique to Black people in the United States. Sexual stereotypes in systemically racist institutions differ depending on the racial/ethnic group in question and stem from unique, if closely related, histories of colonialism and oppression. Furthermore, research into the intersections of multiple racial/ethnic identities can also provide useful insight into the role of racialized gender oppression in the criminal legal system. For example, one can analyze the unique experiences of Afro-Latine, trans sex workers.

Above all else, it is my intent that this research encourage others to adopt intersectional, feminist lenses as they examine the criminal legal system and other dominant institutions, as well as embrace abolitionist perspectives and strategies. As Davis and colleagues (2022) assert, Black feminist and abolitionist frameworks must be utilized alongside each other because the goals of one cannot be fully realized without also attaining the goals of the other. Without abolitionist thought, intersectional, Black feminism functions to reform the criminal legal system while still leaving it intact as a regulatory mechanism for social control. An abolitionist approach without Black feminist thought lacks a pluralist perspective that accounts for diversity of possible social formations, therefore leaving it vulnerable to creating systems that reinforce hierarchical formations in lieu of the criminal legal system. As such, I urge readers and future researchers to understand the confluence of Black feminist and abolitionist frameworks as a necessary precondition to the attainment of rights and freedoms for Black people, trans people, and sex workers alike.

www.ingramcontent.com/pod-product-compliance
Lightning Source LLC
LaVergne TN
LVHW090415210926
848480LV00002B/570
9798348319885